Guides to Straight Thinking

With 13 Common Fallacies

STUART CHASE

Guides to
Straight Thinking

With 13 Common Fallacies

Harper & Row, Publishers
New York, Evanston, and London

Contents

Foreword

"That was a fine speech the Senator made!"

"I didn't think much of it; they say he never went beyond grade school."

What is wrong with this argument? It is a sample of the logical fallacy known as *ad hominem,* where the issue is deserted to attack the character of the person who raises it. By undermining the Senator personally, his critic hopes to discredit the theme of his speech. *Ad hominem* is one of the most common, as well as one of the most ancient, fallacies, and everyone who argues is tempted by it. The Greeks were aware of it, if not Methuselah.

I had long been wondering why we go on falling into this ancient mantrap, when arrangements were made with a group of editors of the *Reader's Digest* for me to develop a series of articles on logical fallacies. The articles the *Digest* carried were well received, and I decided to complete the list and make them into a book, together with some background material and plenty of timely applications.

The study continues my interest in communication and semantics, which dates back to *The Tyranny of Words,* published in 1938, and containing a chapter on logic. The present book is written for people like myself who have been thrown for a loss in trying to understand formal expositions of logic—such, for instance, as the twenty-four-page disquisition in the Fourteenth Edition of the *Encyclopaedia Britannica.* At the same time we have felt a real need for sharper tools in reasoning, and have wondered what the logicians might do to aid us.

Well, there is plenty they can do, especially in the identification of fallacies like *ad hominem*. My study is for the journeyman thinker who would like to know more precisely what the Senator on the floor, the critic of the Senator, the writers of editorials, the omniscient voices on the radio, the attorney in the courtroom, the campaign orators, the copy writers of Madison Avenue, and the Moscow propaganda mill, are trying to make him believe. What is the real meaning behind the rhetoric and the sales talk?

Identifying fallacies, like crossword puzzles, can be an interesting game for active minds, but it is a good deal more than that, especially when applied to analyzing one's own mental processes. As the world becomes more complicated, and the mass media more shrill and insistent, the necessity for straight thinking increases. Homo sapiens is now in so many jams that only a vigorous use of his brains can extricate him—economic jams, racial and religious conflicts, cold wars, population problems—to say nothing of traffic jams.

Fortunately there seems to be little the matter with the human brain as an instrument of thought. Physiologists calculate it contains some twelve to fifteen billion electrical connections, which makes it capable of handling very complicated matters indeed. They estimate that, to duplicate its performance, an electronic computer would have to be a block long and would need all the water of Niagara Falls to cool it. One difficulty is that emotional drives get in the way of efficient use, and some of the fallacies we will examine arise directly from this fact. Another difficulty is lack of mental exercise.

Though the brain, with its marvelous mechanisms for storing memories, will perform thousands of tasks for us without troubling our consciousness, when it comes to analyzing a problem, conscious mental effort must go to work in a process which is always new. No electronic computer, furthermore, can ever grapple with a problem until some human mind has first cleared the ground—"taped it," to use the electronic lingo. Computers can do problems faster than a man, *after* a man has built the problem into them.

The reader will find for reference, in the Appendix, a list of twenty-two classical fallacies developed by students of logic since Aristotle's time. Some are highly technical, applying chiefly to the manipulation of the syllogism. Some overlap each other, some are pretty ambiguous. Authorities differ on the number and classification of fallacies. In addition to those which I have selected for their usefulness today, like *ad hominem,* I have included in my study several derived from modern science. Thirteen fallacies have thus been identified for analysis, with a chapter given to each. We will also look at other examples of false reasoning in the chapters dealing with propaganda and the courtroom.

My study is not a textbook, or a competitor for the standard course in logic—though it might be of use as collateral reading. No student could pass a standard examination if it were his only source. Logic in the colleges and schools, whether "formal" or not, has become formalized. It requires far more attention to technical rules than will be found here. So do not look for the mental pinwheels which philosophers use to dazzle us and each other. The cases you will find are not puzzles, even if some can be made into games. On the contrary, I have tried to make the material as clear as possible for the busy, and sometimes uneasy, consumer of ideas.

The reader will find a large number of stories and illustrations, collected from all over. I have drawn from my own experience, and my wife, who has collaborated closely, has drawn from hers—in a recent stretch of jury duty, for instance, where she found fallacies falling like snow in January. Cases have come from books, magazines, news stories, advertising and publicity matter; from commentator and columnist, and letters to the editor—the last a veritable gold mine. I have also borrowed stories from the books on logic which appear in the Bibliography, and hereby tender my grateful thanks to their authors.

In selecting illustrations from current politics, I shall doubtless be charged with quoting more bad logic by conservatives than by liberals. As I am constitutionally of a liberal turn of mind, the charge probably has merit. But the reader will note also a fair number of cases where New Dealers, Democrats, One Worlders, and reformers of various stripes have been caught out of bounds.

I am indebted to my friend Ernest Angell, the New York attorney, for a critical reading of the chapter on the courtroom, and to Dr. J. G. Brennan of Barnard College, Columbia University, for reviewing the whole manuscript from the point of view of a technical expert in logic. Neither is responsible for the final draft. I am grateful for efficient secretarial help by my neighbors Christine Loring and Lola Donnell.

STUART CHASE

Redding, Connecticut, April, 1956

Guides to
Straight Thinking

With 13 Common Fallacies

Logical principles . . . are inescapable, because any attempt to disregard them reduces our thoughts and words to confusion and gibberish.

MORRIS R. COHEN and ERNEST NAGEL
(in *Logic and Scientific Method*)

Man longs for causes, and the weaker minds, unable to restrain their longing, often barter, for the most sorry theoretic pottage, the truth which patient enquiry would make their own.

JOHN TYNDALL

1

The Logical Animal

It was Bernard Shaw who said that we use our reason only to support our prejudices. This is what psychologists call rationalizing: finding logical reasons for doing what we want to do, or are going to do anyway. Shaw's epigram draws blood, but fortunately for the human race it is not true, at least not universally. All of us rationalize part of the time, but when we stretch it to *all* the time, the moment has arrived to call in a good psychiatrist.

Sane people have their objective intervals, when they manage to deal directly with the world around them and to use that extraordinary instrument the human brain to discover what is actually going on out there. One name for this effort is common sense, another, the objective view, and another more recent name, the scientific attitude. It consists of putting two and two together regardless of one's desires and prejudices. Personal goals and drives do not have to be pursued all the time.

The two-and-two exercise employs reason or logic. Here are the facts, and here are logical conclusions to be drawn from them. Here is the gun with a left thumbprint on the barrel; here is the left thumbprint of Mr. X, identical thereto. It is highly probable that the murderer has been found. Again, a skilled paleontologist may be able to deduce from a jawbone the sex, height, and physical characteristics of an individual who expired ten thousand years ago. A garage mechanic can often tell what is wrong from the sound of your engine; electricians and

1

plumbers constantly solve problems in logic which baffle the average householder—though the householder might learn to solve them if he had the time. Most of us, however, would not find it easy to learn the logic demanded in "taping" the program of an electronic computer.

Ever since Homo sapiens came down from trees he has been using logic to avoid extinction. Often it has failed him most dismally, but success has been more frequent than failure, or we should not be here to speculate about it. "If man," says F. C. S. Schiller, "had not succeeded in devising forms of thought which were applicable to reality he would either have perished, or have adjusted himself in other ways than by the use of intelligence."

One of our Stone Age ancestors comes to an abrupt halt in the forest. He looks again and says to his companion: "That footprint in the mud beside the trail looks like a bear's! It is fresh. It is headed for our water hole. We'd better stay away from the spring, and build a trap just about here!" He has observed three facts—the footprint, its timing, its direction; and he deduces a conclusion of considerable value to his survival. If he were very thirsty he might attempt a rationalization, say that the bear had gone away—but it wouldn't be healthy.

Man, while a relatively large mammal, is singularly unarmored in the matter of teeth, claws, hide, and strength of hug. He cannot run very fast compared to a deer, or hit very hard compared to a gorilla. *He has to use his wits.* Logic, reason, thinking, using one's wits, are nearly synonymous terms, and widely celebrated as the activity which marks men off from all other creatures. This is expressed normally through language, as it is well established that the higher levels of thought are difficult if not impossible without words. A thought may come from the blue, but in order to think about that thought, or especially to discuss it with one's fellows, words are necessary.

I can condition my cat not to jump on the dining room table, but I cannot explain to him why he shouldn't. Animals lack the machinery to pass knowledge down to the next generation, and the next; they have to begin over with each generation. They have no words to describe what they have learned, no method to accumulate the arts and the sciences. A rat may learn to thread a maze for food, but it cannot tell another rat how to do it.

On all levels, logic is very closely related to language, and it is hard to know where one stops and the other begins. "Logos" is Greek for "word," and our "logic" and also the "ologies" of the sciences (archeology, physiology) derive from it.

SOME DEFINITIONS OF LOGIC

Few thinkers have thought about the logical process more intensively than the late Morris R. Cohen. He had the great advantage, furthermore, of familiarity with the logic of modern science and modern mathematics, which were of course unknown in Aristotle's time. His book, *Logic and the Scientific Method*, written with Ernest Nagel, will be our major guide in matters of theory in the pages to come. He says:

Logic is correct reasoning. To be logical is to argue reasonably. By means of logic we can find out what follows if we accept a given statement as true.

And again:

Logic may be said to be concerned with the question of the adequacy of different kinds of evidence. Traditionally, however, it has devoted itself in the main to the study of what constitutes proof, that is, complete or conclusive evidence.

The first definition is the broader. It fits the mental process of our Stone Age ancestor as he spots the spoor of the bear. It is the common or garden logic in use by competent members of the race for half a million years. We all use it many times a day, in the lucid intervals between our emotional behavior and our rationalizations.

Cohen's second definition is more strict, concerned with the subject "logic" as taught in schools and colleges, beginning with the Lyceum of Aristotle. By and large we shall follow the first definition in this book, the logic of everyday living, of common sense, of getting the facts and figuring out what they mean and how best to deal with them.

IT BEGINS EARLY

It is fascinating to observe the logical process developing in young children. Not long ago I was playing chess with my grandson when his sister Anne, aged seven, came over to watch us. She was curious about the pieces, and I stopped a moment to tell her their names.

"The castle is much smaller than the king, but it ought to be bigger," she said.

"Why?" I asked in some perplexity.

"Because the way it is now the king couldn't get into it."

This, I submit, is not the bright saying of a moppet to be laughed at indulgently; it is the human mind beginning to work on a problem of relationships.

A simple statement of fact is not logical or illogical by itself, though it can be true or false or in between. *Only when we draw a conclusion from the statement does logic technically enter.* It is a fact that the castle on a chess board is smaller than the king. It is a fact that kings, in storybooks at least, live in castles. Therefore castles must be larger than kings. Anne put those two facts together to draw a reasonable conclusion.

"The moon is made of green cheese," is a highly improbable statement—though nobody has yet been to the moon to check it. Let us assume it to be true. If you then say: "When our space ship lands we can replenish our food supply," the logic is sound and the conclusion valid. But if, from the same premise, you say: "When our space ship lands we'll find plenty of carbon monoxide," the conclusion does not follow. There is no connection between green cheese and carbon monoxide in this frame of reference.

The point here is of the first importance, and is often misunderstood. Let me restate it.

Logic is the process of drawing a conclusion from one or more statements or propositions, called premises.

If the premises are assumed to be true—whether they are or not—the logic can be technically correct.

Even if the premises are demonstrably true, the logic can be bad. If you say: "There is practically no air on the moon," you are stating a scientific fact.[1] But if you continue: "Therefore the moon is drawing closer to the earth," the conclusion has no relation to the fact, and is illogical.

"Your religion is different from mine." A fact.

"Therefore you are no good." An illogical conclusion—but one held, alas, by untold millions.

"If people live in Connecticut they live in the U.S.A." A fact.

"Therefore if they do not live in the U.S.A. they cannot live in Connecticut." A logical conclusion depending on relationship, like Anne's kings and castles.

Logical as it is to conclude that *if* the moon is made of green cheese we can use it as a grocery store, it makes most of us uneasy—the premise is so wildly improbable. Straight thinking requires more than a logical inference; the facts must also make some sense. If we are going to argue about the moon, we should follow what scientists have discovered about its struc-

[1] Estimated at one million millionth of earth's air at sea level.

ture. Green cheese is definitely out, while lack of an atmosphere is definitely in.

"BECAUSE"

When you hear the word *because,* you can be fairly sure that an exercise in logic is about to take place. The logic may be good, bad, or indifferent, but the person saying "This is so, *because*" is going through the motions of the logical animal. "Castles should be bigger than kings *because* kings have to live in them." In one sense, the study of logic is nothing but an analysis of *becauses*. Logical fallacies occur when the *because* does not follow, does not make sense. Sound logic occurs when it does—though sometimes, as in the fallacy of "arguing in circles" (Chapter 14), it takes quite a bit of triangulation to locate the nonsense. Here is a statement supported by four *becauses*, all wrong:

> The earth is flat. Why?
> *Because* it looks flat.
> *Because* people would fall off the underside if it were a ball.
> *Because* the gods say it is.
> *Because* my father told me so.

Morris Cohen gives us a more sophisticated example: "The number of inhabitants in New York City is greater than the number of hairs on the head of any inhabitant."

How come?

Because tests show that there are never more than five thousand human hairs to a square centimeter. No human head has more than a thousand square centimeters of hair. The limit on any head is thus five million hairs. There are eight million people in New York City. Therefore, there are more people than hairs on any one head. We can also deduce from the above facts that at least two individuals in New York have precisely the same number of hairs on their heads.

I have bathroom scales and I have a cat. I want to weigh the cat. My mind goes to work imagining various complicated basketry constructs to hold the cat on the platform. I try some of them, with a lamentable lack of success; a cat seems to get out of anything at about the speed of light. Then the solution comes—a solution which the alert reader doubtless glimpsed at once. I take the cat in my arms and weigh us both. I drop the cat and weigh myself, and subtract the second reading from the first. . . . This illustrates what is meant by everyday logic, the homely problems constantly demanding a solution on a level above trial and error.

HERODOTUS AND THE NILE

The great historian Herodotus was curious about the Nile Why did it overflow its banks every summer? The facts were clear. Beginning in mid-June, the river flooded back to as much as two days' journey inland, for a period of about three months. "I made every inquiry," said Herodotus, "from priest and peasant, but nobody knew why." He then considers three theories which had been advanced.

First, northwest winds from the Mediterranean backed the river up. This he dismisses because other rivers subjected to the same winds did not back up.

Second, the Nile is an exceptional river and flows from the ocean upstream. Not tenable, says Herodotus; rivers always flow downhill.

Third, melting snows cause the overflow. This sounds plausible, observes Herodotus, but it can't be true. Why? *Because* the Nile flows north from a region hotter than Egypt, where birds fly to spend the winter. Can one find snow in such a torrid country?

Herodotus dismissed all three hypotheses. His logic was keen; no man of his time could have reasoned better. The

trouble was that no traveler had yet visited the sources of the
Nile to report the great snowfields in Ethiopia, or Mt. Ruwenzori,
which lies close to the equator. The third theory was the right
one, but Herodotus' world lacked the knowledge to support it.

This story forcefully illustrates a serious limitation of logic.
One of the most profound thinkers of his time, exercising his
mind to the utmost, was unable to reach the right conclusion
by logic alone. Heavy thinkers down the ages have believed
that if they only sat still and thought hard enough, the right
answer would come. Sometimes it did and often it didn't. Now
we know that unless we heave out of our armchairs and do the
essential leg work or laboratory work, new knowledge seldom
comes.

*First, nail down your facts, get your premises in line with
current knowledge. Second, exercise logic upon them.* Then
you are likely to have a conclusion worth battling for.

The fly-and-bicycle story is a good exercise in simple logic.
You probably remember it. Two cyclists begin to pedal toward
each other at the same moment. They are thirty miles apart
and their rates are equal, fifteen miles per hour. Simultaneously
a fly takes off from A's handlebar to B's handlebar, and back
to A's, in an ever-decreasing round trip. The fly's rate is forty
miles an hour—with no allowance for stops and starts. When
the cyclists meet, the hard-working fly is crushed between the
handlebars. How far has the fly flown?

On first hearing this story some engineers are said to whip
out their slide rules, some mathematicians to exercise their
calculus. Most laymen demand pencil and paper and time to
figure. Others get the answer at once, by eliminating the non-
essential facts. How long before A and B meet? One hour, of
course. Therefore, the fly has flown nonstop for an hour. Therefore, at forty miles per hour, it has flown forty miles. Q.E.D.
Observe that this problem could not be stated, let alone be

solved, without words or other symbols, and that the brightest chimpanzee could make nothing of it, although bright chimpanzees can ride bicycles.

LEVELS OF LOGIC

Up to a century ago or so, people who did not pay their debts were thrown into prison. The logic on one level was inescapable.

> People who won't pay their debts must be punished.
> Jones won't pay his debts. (Usually Jones couldn't.)
> Therefore he must be punished.
> How do we punish civil offenders?
> By putting them in jail.

All very neat and tidy. But on another level the logic was so bad that the whole process had to be abandoned. Poor debtors in prison had no way to work off their debts, and were a burden to taxpayers as well. Nowadays we let them go through bankruptcy proceedings, which wipes out the debt and may hurt their self-respect. Sometimes the bankrupt goes to work and pays off his debt as a matter of honor. This marked improvement in logic, observe, comes from considering more facts about the total situation.

On a cold winter day in the depths of the Great Depression, bulldozers descended on a shanty colony of unemployed men in New York, to clear the area for a new building. The poor starvelings were driven from their tar-paper shacks. It was sad, even cruel, but obviously nothing could be done about it. To give them a dole, in the logic of the year 1931, would have established a dangerous precedent. Said Thurman Arnold, who tells the story: "The eviction of these unfortunates was a symbol of a faith that economic competence can only be developed by refusing to protect incompetence." A lesson, however, painful, had to be taught.

As the work proceeded, two men were discovered unconscious under one of the huts. Instantly the old logic went by the
board and a happier one took its place. It was no longer wrong
to protect citizens from their own incompetence. Twenty
thousand dollars' worth of ambulances, stretchers, pulmotors,
drugs, accompanied by a squad of internes and nurses, rushed
to the scene. The starving men were taken to a hospital and
given treatment which a millionaire could not have afforded
fifty years earlier. "Thus a practical and humanitarian attitude
develops techniques and not logical arguments." Or, to put it
another way, it raises the level of the logic.

RATIONALIZING

D. S. Robinson quotes the "philosophy of an airman" as a
lively example of rationalizing.[2] Rationalizing, as noted earlier,
is logic employed to bolster one's hopes, desires or prejudices.
A flier really has nothing to worry about, for look:

If you fly well there is nothing to worry about.
If you go into a spin, then one of two things can happen: Either
you crash or you don't.
If you don't crash, there is nothing to worry about.
If you do crash, one of two things can happen: Either you are
hurt or you are not hurt.
If you are not hurt, there is nothing to worry about.
If you are badly hurt, one of two things can happen: Either you
recover or you don't.
If you recover there is nothing to worry about.
If you don't recover you can't worry!

One hates to spoil a good story, but if you do recover and
are crippled for life, there is plenty to worry about. Rationalization usually has a catch in it.

[2] In his *Principles of Reasoning.*

SEVEN FIELDS OF LOGIC

Reason enters every human activity, with seven kinds particularly noticeable. Often the logic is faulty but the attempt is there.

1. *Common sense.*

This workaday logic has been practiced constantly by every sane person since time out of mind. He may be alone as he reasons, or in a group. He may or may not use words. The logic, such as it is, is applied to his acts, to his evaluation of himself, his neighbors, and his world.

2. *Formal logic.*

This is a scholarly discipline introduced by Aristotle. At one time wise men believed that through formal logic we could find all the laws governing human thought. Now we know that this task belongs in great part to the social sciences, especially psychology. Aristotle's logic operates through a device called the syllogism, which has its merits; but if followed too rigorously, it can get the straight thinker into trouble. The syllogism was used by the Greeks and the Schoolmen of the Middle Ages to "prove" the most improbable things—for instance, that Achilles could not overtake the tortoise in a race. Nowadays, however, a new streamlined formal logic, also highly technical, goes far beyond the syllogism.

3. *Mathematics.*

Mathematics is chiefly systematized logic. Pure mathematics, hitched to no specific fact—no tons of freight, or years, or temperatures—is incapable of discovering new knowledge. Applied to the physical universe, it can be immensely valuable, aiding the mind when it grows dizzy trying to understand too many events at once. A super-mind might see the relationships at a glance and not need the help of mathematics, but such minds lie far in the biological future. Even Einstein had to use mathematics to help him think.

4. *The logic of modern science.*

Scientists today use not only mathematics but many other logical techniques as well. The techniques include: the verification of hypotheses, continual check between logical inferences and relevant facts, thinking in terms of probability, of processes, of relationships. Scientists employ techniques of modern symbolic logic, including multi-valued systems.

5. *Legal procedure.*

A courtroom is a kind of laboratory of logic, to determine what is evidence and what is not, and whether the defendant is guilty as charged. Smart attorneys try to twist the logic to the advantage of their clients, while the judge tries to keep the argument undistorted. We recall the attorney who said to the jury after summing up his case: "These, gentlemen, are the conclusions upon which I base my facts"—which is the logical process upside down!

6. *Winning arguments, votes, and customers.*

In this area logic is stretched to throw advantage to a special side or interest, but the audience is forewarned. A college debate bristles with *becauses*, but few take it as the serious pursuit of truth; one side is out to win, as in a football game. The debater who argues for the affirmative may switch to the negative in a later contest, and so exercise his mental muscles.

Few sophisticated voters expect the logic of a political campaign to have much connection with reality. When a candidate named Adlai Stevenson tried to make the connection, professionals were alarmed. Wendell Willkie, caught in an inconsistency in the 1940 presidential campaign, dismissed it as "just campaign oratory."

Advertising campaigns are on a still lower level. Sometimes they give us useful information about new products, but mostly they are a verbal stew of half truths, reiteration, snob appeal, and *non-sequiturs,* reinforced with bathing beauties and jingles from the folklore.

7. *All-out propaganda.*

In this final area the distortion of logic goes beyond that normally found in number 6, often to the point of treachery and crime. The reasoning process is twisted, slanted, adulterated, as a matter of course, by demagogues, dictators, and fanatical ideologists. The bigger the misrepresentation one can get away with, the greater the triumph. Logical fallacies are deliberately manipulated, and new mantraps added, such as the "scapegoat" technique. The logic is always two-valued: We are absolutely right and you are absolutely wrong, and anybody in the middle is wrong too. The issue has already been decided by the propagandist; there is no common search for truth.

My classification above, rough as it is, suggests how the exercise of reason pervades human affairs. This book will try to promote the use especially of number 4, scientific reasoning, and to give the reader some defense against numbers 6 and 7—campaign oratory, competitive advertising, and all-out propaganda.

Let us now observe briefly how the study of logic began, some twenty-five hundred years ago.

2

The Greeks Discover Logic

THE GREEKS were the first to investigate how the human mind works; earlier peoples seem to have taken it for granted. The city states of the Aegean in the fifth century B.C. were shaking off their tyrants and dictators and developing democracy. It was not the political system we know today, where every adult has a vote, but a kind of top-drawer democracy for free citizens only. As slaves constituted the great majority of the population, the voters were a relatively small elite group. Slaves did all the manual work, giving their masters plenty of time to think about thinking. The arrangement had its advantages, but also its defects. The voters did not often use their hands to check their thoughts; they tended to neglect first-hand observation, research, and experiment. They were saved, says James Harvey Robinson, "from fumbling with the everyday processes of life."

Citizens met in popular assemblies and forums to discuss civic problems. In Athens, not only political but legal issues were decided in public forums, and the arts of persuasion were increasingly in demand. A school of philosophers called the *Sophists* undertook to develop and standardize those arts. They established academies to teach young Greeks how to argue, win debates and legal cases, get elected to public office. Indeed, the Sophists concentrated so vigorously on techniques for selling an idea that a cloud hangs over their school today, as reflected in our word "sophistry." They might be called the Madison Avenue boys of 400 B.C., specializing in the sixth area of logic, as listed on page 12.

Plato rebuked them. The Sophists, he said, were perfecting specious arguments just to win a case; they made "the worse appear the better reason." Plato seems to have been an early discoverer and exposer of logical fallacies, and once exclaimed, in *Protagoras:*

> ... We must take care, my friend, that the Sophist does not deceive us when he praises what he sells, like the dealers . . . who sell the food of the body; for they praise indiscriminately all their goods. . . . In like manner those who carry about the wares of knowledge, and make the round of the cities, and sell them to any customer who is in want of them, praise them all alike. . . .

Socrates, meanwhile, had defined cross-examination, and stimulated the art of "dialectics," meaning the elaboration of ideas through keen, intelligent discussion. We encounter here two contrasting uses of logic as developed by Greek thinkers —uses still in sharp contrast today. The Sophists employed the new knowledge to win a case, and to "praise indiscriminately"; Socrates employed it to thresh out an issue and reach a dependable conclusion. The first was an attempt to advance somebody's power or position, the second to advance human knowledge.

ARISTOTLE'S FORMAL LOGIC

The Sophists, Socrates, Plato, speculated widely and often deeply about the reasoning process, but it remained for Aristotle boldly to develop the laws of thought, with the syllogism as a supporting tool. He was born at Stagira, a Greek colonial city on the coast of Macedonia, in 384 B.C. His father, a doctor, may have aroused his interest in philosophy. At the age of seventeen he went to Athens to become a pupil of Plato, and remained there until the master's death twenty years later.

He then wandered about the Aegean, observing and teaching. For a time he acted as tutor to the young Alexander, son of King Philip of Macedon. When Alexander succeeded to the throne, Aristotle went back to Athens to organize and head his famous Lyceum. Some Greeks called it the "peripatetic" school, because Aristotle walked up and down as he talked with his pupils. Here, in the last dozen years of his life, he wrote the great treatises on politics, physics, ethics, and logic. Much of his work has been lost; what has come down to us shows the stature of his mind, and his consuming desire to know and understand.

THE LAWS OF THOUGHT

Words are slippery in any language. To prove a proposition absolutely by words alone has never been easy. Aristotle developed a method by which he hoped words could be kept in order, and proof made watertight.

He used the verb "to be" (in Greek, of course) to divide any subject, even the entire cosmos, into a region called "A," and a region called "not-A." In discussion, he said, we must distinguish carefully between these regions. This thesis was summarized by his disciples in three laws, which at first reading seem almost too simple to be important. They stem, however, from profound cogitation by perhaps the foremost philosopher of ancient Greece, and have influenced the culture and thought of all the Western world. Here they are:[1]

1. *The law of identity* affirms that A is A, or that every event and every judgment is identical with itself.

2. *The law of contradiction* affirms that A cannot both be A and not be A.

3. *The law of the excluded middle* affirms that everything must be either A or not-A.

"Aristotle," says Schiller, "explicitly recognizes the laws of

---

[1] Following F. C. S. Schiller, *Formal Logic.*

contradiction and excluded middle, and implicitly that of identity." The master clearly showed, however, that he was aware that these principles were not absolutes but had some flexibility.

In the hands of some of his followers the three principles have taken on a grim finality, inflexible and absolute. The law of identity, rigidly interpreted, does not allow for changes in A through time, or for the differing meanings which can be attached to A. "A rose is a rose," but a rose in June is not identical with the same rose in September, so far as color, scent, and structure go. Webster's recent college dictionary gives the word "science" six different meanings, ending up with Christian Science. To say that "science is science and let's have no more nonsense about it" is a nonsensical statement. To which meaning do you refer? The law of identity, inflexibly interpreted, runs head on into the "one proper meaning superstition," which modern students of communication and language most properly condemn.

The laws of contradiction and excluded middle, in the hands of some Aristotelians, have congealed into a mental fixation where an event must be either black or white, with no room for shades of gray. So interpreted, the law of contradiction says that nothing can be both "good" and "bad," both "poisonous" and "beneficial." But such drugs as arsenic, belladonna, curare, can be beneficial in small doses, though lethal in large. And what about a friend of mine who has an allergy for fresh eggs, and becomes deathly ill if he eats one?

The third law, that of the excluded middle, rigidly interpreted, supports the slogan that "those who are not with us are against us." Applied to American foreign policy today, such thinking would throw all the neutral nations, like India and Burma, into the Communist camp—a pretty disastrous line to take.[2]

[2] See Chapter 16 for an analysis of some dangers of two-valued thinking.

THE SYLLOGISM

Aristotle also developed a verbal device called the *syllogism,* hoping it could be used to demonstrate absolute proof. Experience has not borne him out. Used with a safety lock, however, the syllogism can be helpful. I shall use it, for instance, in Chapter 17, to analyze the fallacious logic of "guilt by association."

A syllogism is a combination of three propositions called: (1) the major premise, (2) the minor premise, and (3) the conclusion. Applying these labels to the classic syllogism found in all the textbooks:

All men are mortal—the major premise.
Socrates is a man—the minor premise.
Therefore Socrates is mortal—the conclusion.

Observe that both these premises are statements of fact, while the conclusion is the result of logic applied to the facts. The logic, moreover, is as automatic as a slot machine. "Mortal" is the so-called major term of the syllogism. (We must be careful not to confuse the major *term* with the major *premise.*) "Man" is the so-called middle term. "Socrates" is the minor term. When the button is pushed to get the conclusion, the middle term, "man," drops down the chute, leaving Socrates equated with mortality.

This is reasonably simple, but Aristotelians, starting with the mortality of Socrates, can take us over some pretty rough terrain. For these maneuvers we refer the reader to the special treatises on logic, some of which are listed in the Bibliography. To give an idea of the complications, there are four possible "figures" in the syllogism, while each figure is capable of sixty-four "moods." This produces a total of 256 possible forms which a syllogism may take. We are relieved to hear, however, that the theoretical total is sharply curtailed by the application of eight rules. (The first rule, for instance, is that a syllogism must not contain more than three terms.)

TWO THOUSAND YEARS

The syllogism and the laws of thought were high points of the classical inquiry into the workings of the mind. The Greek Lyceum went on into Roman times, but its scholars were content to repeat, with a few marginal notes, the ideas of the master. Aristotle's formal logic became a "self-sealing" doctrine, beyond all criticism and amendment. Meanwhile, of course, common sense logic flourished as usual in the interest of survival. The Romans used the latter constantly in their many political problems of conquering and administering an empire. The Romans were not primarily philosophers, or much interested in the process of thinking as such. The Emperor Justinian closed the Lyceum in A.D. 529.

In the twelfth century, Aristotle was rediscovered in Europe through Arab translation, and presently achieved a towering reputation. He became *the* philosopher. Christian, Arab, and Jewish scholars strove to harmonize their respective theologies with his texts. Medieval scholasticism, a hybrid between Aristotelian logic and theology, erected a formidable apparatus to defend theological doctrines against the beliefs of pagan without and heretic within.

Not much new knowledge was discovered. The human brain of course was as good as ever, but it turned in upon itself. Knights in armor on the tournament field toppled one another from their chargers, while inside the universities dialecticians in another kind of tournament toppled one another from their logical positions. Lord Bacon says of them in a famous passage:

Having sharp and strong wits, and abundance of leisure . . . their wits being shut up in the cells of a few authors, as their persons were shut up in the cells of monasteries and colleges, and knowing little history either of nature or time, they did . . . spin out unto us those laborious webs of learning. . . .

The laborious webs of learning could also be put to grim uses. In A.D. 1300, unless one manipulated his dialectics carefully, he might be mistaken for a "materialist," and argue himself into a pot of boiling oil. George Moore, in *Héloise and Abélard*, gives some frightening examples of medieval logic-chopping.

Not all the output of the "sharp and strong wits" has been translated for modern inspection, and perhaps it is unjust to accuse the Schoolmen of only regurgitating knowledge without advancing it. One thing they did of great value to our study; they worked out and named the classical list of logical fallacies.[3] Some of the Latin names like *ad hominem* and *post hoc* are still in lively use today.

WORD TROUBLE

The logic of the Greeks as well as that of the Schoolmen suffered from the confusion of words with things. It had no proper conception of the function of abstract terms, as worked out by modern linguists and semanticists. The classicists do not seem to have been much interested in finding the referents to which their words referred; they began their powerful reasoning with the term itself.

When they used the word "goodness" they apparently believed that there was an essence, an entity, out in the world somewhere, a veritable package of goodness which gave meaning to the word. Today we know that "goodness" is an abstraction in our heads. Each one of us, as we view events, labels some of them good, and some not so good, with wide areas of disagreement. Consider, for instance, the differing images in people's minds of Franklin D. Roosevelt, and the resulting estimates of his "goodness."

[3] See Appendix.

Plato, after taking the Sophists sternly to task, got into serious difficulty by confusing words with things. In one of his loftiest flights, says Schiller, Plato "conceived the grandiose fancy of a supreme 'Idea of the Good' from which all the other 'Ideas' were to be deduced, thereby rendering all knowledge accessible at one stroke. In other words, all the Laws of Nature were to be 'explained' by being derived from a single law, which was to be the Universal Key to the whole intelligible world."

There were very few in the Greek world to devise the practical apparatus by which, in combination with reason, knowledge grows. The lens had not been invented, and no telescopes or microscopes were available to verify hypotheses—as the Royal Society today can verify Einstein's hypotheses. There were no clocks, thermometers, barometers, cameras, mariner's compasses, spectroscopes, stethoscopes. Worse still, there was no suitable numerical system with which to take readings. The Arabs did not present the world with the decimal system and its priceless zero for another fifteen hundred years. Archimedes, to be sure, was a rare man with his hands, but he disdained to make any records of his ingenious devices, says James Harvey Robinson, "as being unworthy of the noble profession of a philosopher."

FOUR REASONS FOR THE DEAD END

Why did the study of how we think, begun so brilliantly by the philosophers of Greece, stay pretty much on dead center for two thousand years? One reason was certainly the lack of physical experiments and proper instruments to check conclusions. Another was the confusion of words with things, the belief that if a word was there, a corresponding essence or entity must be there too.

John Dewey emphasizes a third and allied reason when he says: "The ultimate premises of all knowledge were assumed to be already in possession of the mind." The classicists did not appreciate that the human mind is a blank page on which experience is written and evaluated, and that words are meaningless unless they can be related to the experience of the speaker and the hearer. They apparently believed that a rational perception of axioms and self-evident truths was all that was needed to acquire knowledge. If the thinker only *thought* hard enough in the proper categories, truth would stand revealed.

A serious difficulty was that the logic developed by Aristotle's followers had little use for conclusions which were not inevitable and absolute—the slot machine idea. The concept, let alone the mathematics, of *probabilities,* had not been invented. The idea of truth as relative, as probable, as approaching complete certainty but never quite reaching it, seems to have been outside the horizon of the classicists. Yet it is on this foundation that modern science rests, with no limit to its creative progress yet in sight.

Finally it should be emphasized that scholars are still disputing what Aristotle meant in the fragments of his writings which have come down to us,[4] what solid contributions, if any, his followers made, and what precisely was the role of the Schoolmen in developing new ideas. This chapter has had to thread its way with some caution among these disputes and uncertainties.

We can, however, be reasonably sure of three broad conclusions: The Greeks began the objective study of how we think, for which no praise is too high. These studies, however, made little progress for another two thousand years. Modern science, beginning with Galileo's experiments as a convenient date, marked another great surge forward.

[4] A discovery of his complete works would probably outrival the finding of the Dead Sea Scrolls.

3

How Scientists Reason

PLATO began with a universal "idea of the good" and
worked down from there. Galileo reversed the process, starting
with first-hand experience and working up. The famous experiments in which he dropped shot of assorted sizes from the
Leaning Tower of Pisa, timing their fall, proved that the
velocity of freely falling bodies does not depend on weight.
He went on to inquire what it does depend on, which meant
more experiments, and the invention of instruments for closer
observation.

Galileo sought the facts and used his powerful reason on
them. The Schoolmen began and ended with reason. Reason
told them that heavy bodies should fall faster than lighter
bodies, and they could not be bothered with hauling shot to
the tops of towers. Along about A.D. 1400, facts began to receive the right of way in Western thought, and gradually the
great era of modern science opened, the era we are now in
up to our necks.

No single cause can be found for the change. A complex
process seems to have been at work. The Crusades helped
to free communication lines, over which flowed the mathematics and the scientific observations of the Arab world.
Freer communication encouraged freer thinking. Marco Polo
made his way to China, the Portuguese pushed down the west
coast of Africa, Columbus landed in the West Indies. The
explorers and navigators needed instruments to steer by, and

methods for calculating longitude and latitude. Trade followed exploration, with new products and a growing curiosity about the world.

The new knowledge was bitterly resisted in many quarters. Bruno was burned at the stake for dangerous thoughts about religion, and other pioneers, including Galileo himself, were roughly handled. But by 1600 it was safe to investigate the solar system and most material things, as well as energy and motion. The applications of science in navigation, trade, mining, manufactures, were far too valuable to be throttled by syllogisms. Presently Newton arrived at the principles of gravitation, perhaps the greatest synthesis of observation, reason, and verification ever achieved by one human mind.

The exciting story of the rise of science has often been told, and I will not repeat it here. It is symbolized by Galileo. Instead of merely thinking about falling bodies, he went out and dropped some.

The three steps in the scientific method follow naturally: *First*, get together the facts bearing on your question. *Second*, develop a theory, or hypothesis, to explain the facts. *Third*, arrange experiments to verify the hypothesis. Arrange them in such a manner that other competent observers can repeat them. Maintain a healthy skepticism throughout, and be ready to say "I was wrong."

The growth of science in the last four hundred years has been aided by a number of basic concepts and mental tools, largely unknown or ignored in the logic of the ancients. Journeymen thinkers, such as you and I, can take advantage of them, where the journeyman thinker before Galileo had no such opportunity. He had to stick to common sense, or go in for the rigors of the syllogism. You and I, lacking a Ph.D. in physics, may not be able to follow the logic of science all out, but we can use the general approach. We can ask what are the facts, and has the theory been verified? We can keep an open mind until competent observers reach some kind of agreement. We can avoid pounding the table on matters we know little about. Was it Bertrand Russell who said that one's certainty varies inversely with one's knowledge?

To refresh the reader's memory, here is a brief sketch of some of the chief mental tools of modern science, which, consciously or unconsciously, are part of the background of everyone who tries to think rationally today.

PROBABILITIES INSTEAD OF ABSOLUTES

Scientists have become very shy of declaring a thing 100 percent so, though they may settle sometimes for 99.999 percent. The hope is to make a closer and closer fit to nature. Thus Newton greatly refined our knowledge with his laws of gravitation. Einstein corrected Newton in some particulars with the laws of relativity, and made a still closer fit. Physicists today are tightening some of Einstein's concepts, with a big change foreseeable if quantum theory can be reconciled with relativity. Modern scientists find probabilities not only more accurate but more fruitful in the pursuit of knowledge.

This is particularly true in social science, where probabilities are usually lower than in physics. The social and political problems which we argue about lie in this area, and to take a 100 percent position usually ends intelligent discussion. One had better not say: "Russia is going to collapse within six months," but rather: "If the reports on the crisis in Russian agriculture are true, it looks as though the Kremlin would have to change its foreign policy."

Or take the aptitude testing for airplane pilots. The absolutist position would be that a man is a good pilot or he isn't. Social scientists during the war worked out tests for a series of psychological and physical traits. They proved by controlled ex-

periments that a candidate who ranked high in the tests had
about an 80 percent chance of making good on the flying field
—not that the tests were infallible or perfectly correlated with
performance but that the *probability* was high. With tens of
thousands of young men taking the tests, the savings in human
life, to say nothing of the taxpayer's money, were of course
enormous.

MATHEMATICAL THINKING

This concept of probability, which revolutionized science,
originated in repeated throws of dice, with a careful scoring of
results. Upon these results the probability mathematics of
Pascal and Fermat was reared. No earlier civilization had had
more than the rudiments of mathematics to aid in the pursuit
of knowledge. Even the available number systems put a powerful brake on figuring things out. Pity the Roman civil engineer
who, to compute his cuts and fills, had to multiply XLVIII
by CCCXXIV.

Ever since the Arabs introduced the decimal system into
Europe, mathematics has been expanding. Newton, before he
could explain to himself or others what he had found, had to
invent integral calculus. Einstein, of course, did much of his
thinking in the language of mathematics. The gravitational
equations of his general theory of relativity are written in a
form of mathematics called *tensors*. Meanwhile, George Boole
in the nineteenth century invented a new kind of algebra
which applied not to numbers but to relations. It is useful
both to students of logic and to telephone company engineers
planning to expand the dial system.

In modern symbolic logic, instead of manipulating words,
one manipulates symbols, as in algebra. Instead of writing
"All men are mortal," one puts down $a\bar{b} = 0$, and works
through the problem as one involving technical relations be-

tween classes. Symbolic logic has been intensively developed in recent years, to become "a wonderful streamlined mathematical machine."[1]

Meanwhile, two Polish mathematicians, Tarski and Luka-siewics, perfected about 1930 a consistent "multi-valued" logic, which turned out to be much more flexible than some of the older two-valued varieties.

THINKING IN TERMS OF PROCESS

The old logic, because it tends to proceed from a single cause to a given effect, is sometimes called linear thinking. Today scientists find such thinking too limited. A given effect—whether a stomach-ache or a revolution—may be the result of many causes, and in turn produces still further effects. A kind of spiraling *process* appears, with one cause reinforcing another.[2] Or a series of effects may occur, and one tend to block another. In medicine, for instance, a new drug may perform a miracle in clearing up an infection, but break down the body's resistance to other disorders. Similarly, in the field of social science, one should not look for a single cause for juvenile delinquency; various processes are at work, and remedies must be sought accordingly.

THINKING IN RELATIONSHIPS

Einstein in his demonstration of relativity showed that time changes with velocity; the faster you go, the longer the time interval. If you could arrange to travel at the speed of light, 186,000 miles per second, you could theoretically live forever. This conclusion takes us into high-speed physics, but the relativity idea applies all down the line.

[1] Hugh and Lillian Lieber, *Mits, Wits and Logic.*
[2] "Rope reasoning" is a graphic nickname applied to some of these new types of thinking.

A simple illustration to show the relativity of "hot" and "cold" is that of the three pails. Put very cold water in one pail, very hot in another, tepid water in the third. Dip your right hand for a moment in the hot water, then in tepid. How does it feel? *Cold!* Now hold your left hand first in the cold water and then in the tepid. How does it feel? *Hot!* The same pail of water can produce sensations either "hot" or "cold," depending on where your hand has last been. It is the *relation* which counts, rather than any absolute property of "coldness" or "hotness."

OPERATIONAL DEFINITIONS

Those of us who are not mathematicians and experts in symbolic and multi-valued logic find the scientists' "operational definition" especially useful. As described by Bridgman in *The Logic of Modern Physics,* it is a method for defining the terms we use in science, or indeed in any serious discussion. A term which is *not* susceptible to an operational definition usually remains fuzzy, if not completely meaningless. This distinction saves endless hours of debating about things which, while they may sound meaningful enough, can never really be pinned down.

When a scientist, says Bridgman, is asked to define such a term as "length" he does not go to the dictionary; he does not even open his mouth. He performs certain operations with his hands, using clocks or meter sticks or whatever instruments are necessary. The definition grows out of what he *does*: "Look, here is what I mean by length." "Length" turns out to have several meanings, one for stable things like a house, another for moving things like a Greyhound bus, another for stellar distances.

This approach is full of lessons for straight thinkers. *If no operation can be performed, it is highly improbable that two human minds can get close enough to the subject to discuss it intelligently.* A bull session may be amusing, but on such a subject it cannot get much of anywhere. Some scholars do not agree with this assertion; but Bridgman insists it is the only way that physicists can use their reason profitably on many problems. He gives us samples of questions which were meaningless in physics, and are likely to remain so for a long while to come:

> What is the ultimate nature of matter?
> Was there ever a time when matter did not exist?
> Why does time flow?
> May space or time be discontinuous?
> Are there parts of nature forever beyond our detection?
> Is a universe possible in which laws are different?

You can take a carload of meter sticks, stop watches, and Geiger counters, but you will not be able to perform operations to give such questions meaning. So they can be skipped—except in the aforesaid bull sessions.

We can skip many in the field of the social sciences too, using Bridgman's touchstone:

> Is thought possible without language?
> Is environment more important than heredity?
> What is economic value?
> Is his difficulty physical or mental?

We can make guesses about these questions, and perhaps enjoy an interesting give-and-take, but no operation can be performed to give them exact meaning. At least none has yet been found.

THE TOOL OF SEMANTICS

The last technique we shall touch on in this brief review is semantics, defined as "the systematic study of meaning." It is concerned with what a speaker *means* as well as what he says —a point overlooked by many of the classicists. Semantics is only one of a group of disciplines concerned with communication, others being linguistics, cybernetics, perception theory, and so on.[3]

The student of semantics analyzes some of the roadblocks which held up the old logicians. If the giants of the Hellenic world had been more aware of the relativity of language, we might all be further along. Semantics is deeply concerned with the use and abuse of abstract terms. It has invented so-called "abstraction ladders," to indicate how far one's words may be from the concrete event under discussion. Semantics also charts various dangers in two-valued thinking, and in false identification. It can be applied in sifting charges of guilt by association, and guilt by kinship. It is useful too in the analysis of "gobbledygook," the clouding of meaning by fancy language. It is invaluable in analyzing campaign oratory, doubletalk, high-speed propaganda, and the arts of demagogues. It is very helpful in spotting logical fallacies.

Caught in the toils of language, without adequate mathematics, laboratories, instruments, without the concept of probability, process, and relativity, it is remarkable that scientists before Galileo discovered as much as they did, and not at all surprising that philosophers ran off the track from time to time.

Some of us today seem to be content to go along with the Sophists and the Schoolmen, but others are using the logic of modern science to gain a better understanding of our world.

---

[3] My book, *Power of Words,* 1954, describes a dozen disciplines in the field of communication.

4

Finding the Facts

Now THAT we have looked at some modern tools, let us get on to the main business of analyzing logical fallacies. The greatest fallacy of all lies in not following Galileo by going first to the facts. This mistake, however, is so broad and widespread that it hardly belongs with the thirteen more specialized fallacies to be described in the chapters to come.

Failure to find the facts handicaps nearly all discussions of political and social events. Here is a typical example—a conversation I actually overheard. The scene is a New York restaurant off Fifth Avenue at lunch-time. Juan Perón, the dictator of Argentina, has just been deposed, with headlines in all the morning papers. At the next table a distinguished-looking man with a clipped mustache and a charcoal-gray suit is talking to a younger woman with a long ivory cigarette holder. In confident, clearly audible voices, their dialogue develops like this:

"Well," the woman says, "it all goes to show you can't get away with it forever."

"Right," the man says, "and it goes to show you can't buck the Church there or anywhere else."

The woman waves her holder to emphasize her next point. "You can't trust those Latin Americans anyway. They're so emotional; look at the way they drive!"

"Another thing," the man says, "is the labor situation. If Perón hadn't given the unions all that power he might have hung on longer—they always double-cross you."

"As for that Eva Perón," the woman says, "she was a model
or something. He actually tried to make her vice-president!"
Another indignant wave.

"Yes," the man says, "comic opera politics. They call themselves democracies down there, but it's just one dictator after
another."

The conversation, you will note, begins with big, thumping
generalizations, salted with popular prejudices against foreigners. Such stray facts as the couple happen to mention are
of the shakiest character. Neither the man nor the woman appears to know anything definite about Evita Perón, the labor
unions, the Army, the position of the Church, the economic
crisis in Argentina. But both, judging by their voices, believe
that they must keep up with the world, and both—like most
of us who try to think at all—cannot tolerate an explanatory
vacuum. The headlines about the fall of Perón—any big news
story—must be explained now, at once, conclusively and
emphatically! So they throw into the explanatory vacuum some
of the prejudices, homilies, clichés, folk sayings readily available in their minds.

The people at the next table we may be sure have better
minds than that. Let us reconstruct the conversation with the
idea of facts first:

"So Perón is out," the man says.

"Yes, I wonder why." The woman looks really curious.

The man sips his martini. "Complicated," he says. "I haven't
followed it any too carefully, but I'm told the export market
for Argentine beef and wheat is in bad shape. Lately
Perón seems to have developed serious delusions of grandeur,
lost contact with reality. He's been defying the Army, the big
landowners, the Church. Looks like too much for anyone to
take on. The *Times* has a good man in B.A. and his dispatches

ought to help fit the pieces together. I wish we had my friend Carleton Beals here at this table; he's an expert on Latin American politics."

"Why shouldn't Argentina have a real democratic government?" the woman asks. "Wasn't *La Prensa* a great liberal newspaper until Perón suppressed it?"

"That's true," the man says. "Perhaps we can do something now to help Argentina back in the groove. She could be a kind of democratic anchor for the hemisphere in the South."

Such a conversation at the next table would surprise us, but it does not require a pair of giant intellects. It requires a different approach, a search for what is dependably known, a caution against sweeping generalizations, an eye on one's prejudices, and the ability to say "I don't know."

FACTS CONQUER A MOUNTAIN

The first ascent of the Matterhorn in 1865 was more the result of skilful reasoning than of physical agility and endurance. Edward Whymper had assaulted "that awful mountain" seven times on its southwest ridge, where the venture seemed less hopeless than from other points. His party, like every previous climbing party, was always turned back. Once he fell headlong down a snow gully and barely escaped with his life. A serious difficulty was that the rock strata of the southwest ridge sloped downward toward the climber, making footholds precarious.

Whymper cast about for other possible routes. From the Riffelberg above Zermatt, the Matterhorn sends a great rock fang into the sky. The east face from there looks almost perpendicular for thousands of feet, and no guide or observer ever dreamed of an assault from that direction. Whymper, however, noted two facts: *first*, patches of snow lay on the east face throughout the summer, meaning that it was deep. Snow does not cling to perpendicular surfaces; 40 degrees is about its limit. *Second,* the snow etched strata lines in rough parallels that showed the rocks tilted upward, toward the right-hand side of the face.

Therefore, Whymper concluded, the east face could not be as steep as it looked, and if a climber got on its right-hand side, he would find a rock structure like a staircase, instead of one like a coal chute. These deductions of course had to be checked. So he tramped around the base of the Matterhorn to the chalets of Staffel, where the east face with its ridge could be seen in profile. Sure enough, the fang leaned backward, giving a climbing angle of 40 degrees, instead of 90 degrees!

So, defying the massed opinion of the guides and observers, the verdicts of "utterly impossible," and even the evidence of the eye itself from Zermatt, up went Whymper on the east face, like a squirrel up a tree. The Matterhorn was conquered![1]

At the other end of the scale is a U.P. story, covering the 1955 convention of the Daughters of the American Revolution. A resolution was proposed demanding that the United Nations should "cease immediately and completely" from interfering in American affairs. A delegate from Washington spoke against the resolution and said: "Let us observe before we condemn, and send observers to the U. N. to see if rumors of concealed world federalist pressure are true."

Up rose a delegate from Missouri in vigorous support of the resolution. Sending observers to find the facts, said she, would reflect on the dignity of our great organization. "Forget about observing. Let's go after them with clubs and what-have-you like our forefathers!"

WHAT IS A FACT?

A cartoon in *The New Yorker* shows a lady—a very determined-looking lady—in a jury box. She is saying: "I don't listen to the evidence; I like to make up my own mind."

[1] Tragedy came in the descent that same day when the rope broke. But that is another story.

Straight thinkers go first to the facts. Good, but what is a fact? Any department of philosophy worth its salt can spend a couple of semesters on this one. Let us make an end run around the philosophers and pick a definition from the scientists:

A fact is an event in space-time which remains the same from different viewpoints—or, more technically, is invariant under a transformation of axes. In ordinary discussion a fact is invariant as seen by competent observers.

The event should be *located*, if possible, with dates and places, to make it easier to verify. Here are a few different kinds of facts:

1. Material objects or creatures at given places and dates: the maple in my garden in the autumn of 1956; a man named Arthur Gates who last year lived at 214 Main Street; the third broken column from the Temple of the Warriors at Chichen Itza as it lay on the ground before restoration. Also collections of people or objects: all the children in the public schools of Los Angeles in September, 1940; all trailer trucks in operation in the U.S. on April 1, 1955. (Count them.)

2. Happenings at given places and dates: Truman elected President November, 1948; Steamer *Titanic* sinks in North Atlantic, April, 1912; Elizabeth Williams fell on the sidewalk on Thursday last and broke her ankle; an eclipse of the sun was visible in the U.S. in January, 1925; Matterhorn climbed July, 1865. These happenings must be verified at the time by competent witnesses and are usually recorded in some permanent way.

3. Processes verified by observation or experiment: water freezes at 32 degrees Fahrenheit; an injection of adrenalin makes the blood clot more rapidly; etc., etc.

Facts like these are not usually subjects for argument. All competent observers agree too that the moon has almost no atmosphere; that Lee surrendered at Appomattox Court House in April, 1865; that an injection of Salk vaccine diminishes the probability of your child's contracting poliomyelitis; that one part of fluorine to a million parts of drinking water reduces tooth decay. It is impractical, if not impossible, for one individual to round up by first-hand observation all the facts bearing on a big issue—say Perón in Argentina. It is often hard to round them up on even a small issue. As the world becomes more complicated, we must rely on second-hand sources to an increasing degree. Are the sources trustworthy? Have they objective authority behind them? Are the findings up-to-date, or are they clichés worn smooth by repetition?

Reasonable men learn to pick their sources for ideas with at least as much care as they pick their food and clothing. They consult good reference books and often compare them; they choose news services and reporters who follow no party line, reporting the unpleasant news as well as the pleasant, without slant or ideology. On March 13, 1956, the *New York Times* published a magnificent special supplement on the progress of desegregation in the South. Ten top journalists had been assigned to travel through the region and interview citizens and leaders of both races. Said the *Times* editorially: "These reporters were not sent out to pass judgment on the merits of the case; they were sent out to find and report the facts." This approach makes us trust the conclusions of the survey, a survey which you or I could never make alone.

THIRTEEN FALLACIES

Plato, when he rebuked the Sophists, may have founded the art of detecting logical fallacies. The classicists during the succeeding centuries carried on. They worked out many technical fallacies in the mechanics of the syllogism and also, to their credit, a number applicable to ordinary discussion.

My major concern in this book is with the fallacies in

ordinary thinking and discussion to which all of us are prone. I am not so much worried about breaking the rules of the syllogism as about why a given line of reasoning leads into a blind alley. What detour has confused us? How can we get back on the highroad?

After a good deal of study, I have selected thirteen fallacies, or types of false reasoning, to examine in the next thirteen chapters. Some have Latin names, some not. All are common—I have stumbled over every one of them in the past. In each, the reason which follows the term *because,* fails, under analysis, to make sense. Either the facts are inadequate, or the logic is bad, or both. Here they are in bare outline:

1. *Over-generalizing.* Jumping to conclusions from one or two cases.

2. *"Thin entering wedge."* A special type of over-generalizing involving prediction. If this is done, then that—usually dire —will follow.

3. *Getting personal.* Forsaking the issue to attack the character of its defender.

4. *"You're another."* My point may be bad but yours is just as bad, so that makes it quits.

5. *Cause and effect.* If event B comes *after* event A, then it is assumed to be the result of A.

6. *False analogies. This* situation, it is argued, is exactly like *that* situation—but it isn't.

7. *Wise men can be wrong.* Clinching an argument by an appeal to authority.

8. *"Figures prove."* A subclass of the above, especially popular in America today.

9. *Appeal to the crowd.* Distorting an issue with mass prejudices.

10. *Arguing in circles.* Using a conclusion to prove itself.

11. *"Self-evident truths."* Trying to win an argument by saying "everybody knows" it must be true.

12. *Black or white.* Forcing an issue with many aspects into just two sides, and so neglecting important shades of gray.

13. *Guilt by association.* Making a spurious identification between two dissimilar persons or events.

These thirteen by no means exhaust the list. The Appendix contains a reasonably complete list of the classic fallacies. Classic scholars include *appeal to pity, appeal to fear,* and others, which I have omitted as not distinctive enough.

Two classic fallacies, *appeal to ignorance,* and *multiple questions* I will explain in a paragraph or two when we come to the courtroom chapter. They did not seem to demand chapters for themselves in a study of this limited scope.

Big-time propagandists and special pleaders employ all thirteen fallacies when it suits their book, but also use special blockbusters, like the "Big Lie." In developing the thirteen I have had innocent violations more in mind than calculated doubletalk. In all-out propaganda there is no real argument in the Socratic sense. The propagandist has decided the issue in advance and allows no objective discussion. This is it, and his job is to use every psychological trick to force your agreement.

The classicists may have thought that each fallacy they identified and named was entirely different from all the others, that there was no overlapping or interference. No modern student of semantics would assume this. The fallacies listed are different enough to rate different names, but out in the workaday world where we argue and debate, they are constantly straying into one another's territory. Shall we give up the classifications because there is some overlapping? Not at all. The alternative is wading into a vast, yeasty stew of bad arguments, with very little to hold on to.

We badly need the thirteen classes and shall now proceed to use them.

5

Over-generalizing

Fallacy Number One

SECUNDUM QUID

ONE SWALLOW does not make a summer, nor can two or three cases often support a dependable generalization. Yet all of us, including the most polished eggheads, are constantly falling into this mental mantrap. It is the commonest, probably the most seductive, and potentially the most dangerous, of all the fallacies.

You drive through a town and see a drunken man on the sidewalk. A few blocks further on you see another. You turn to your companion: "Nothing but drunks in this town!" Soon you are out in the country, bowling along at fifty. A car passes you as if you were parked. On a curve a second whizzes by. Your companion turns to you: "All the drivers in this state are crazy!" Two thumping generalizations, each built on two cases. If we stop to think, we usually recognize the exaggeration and the unfairness of such generalizations. Trouble comes when we do not stop to think—or when we build them on a prejudice.

This kind of reasoning has been around for a long time. Aristotle was aware of its dangers and called it "reasoning by example," meaning too few examples. What it boils down to is failing to count your swallows before anouncing that summer is here. Driving from my home to New Haven the other day, a distance of about forty miles, I caught myself saying: "Every time I look around I see a new ranch-type house going up." So on the return trip I counted them; there were exactly five under construction. And how many times had I "looked around"? I suppose I had glanced to right and left—as one must at side roads and so forth in driving—several hundred times.

In this fallacy we do not make the error, developed in Chapter 4, of neglecting facts altogether and rushing immediately to the level of opinion. We start at the fact level properly enough, but *we do not stay there*. A case or two and up we go to a rousing over-simplification about drunks, speeders, ranch-style houses—or, more seriously, about foreigners, Negroes, labor leaders, teen-agers.

Over-generalizing takes many forms. It crops out in personal thinking and conversations as above. It is indispensable to those who compose epigrams and wisecracks, and most critics and reviewers find it very handy. It is standard for columnists and commentators who try to compress the complicated news stories of the day "into a nutshell." Newspaper headlines are a continuing exhibit of over-generalizing, but more from typographical necessity than deliberate intent. Cartoonists are under continual temptation. Those persons who go about scenting plots and conspiracies in the most innocent happenings are confirmed addicts, and so are those who follow esoteric cults of all varieties.

STRAW MEN

One vigorous branch is the creation of straw men to represent a class. You take a few stray characteristics, build a dummy around them, and then briskly demolish it. Here, for instance, is a debate between Russell Kirk and Arthur Schlesinger, Jr., on "Conservative vs. Liberal."[1] Mr. Kirk leads off with a picture of a "liberal" which would hardly fit Mr. Schlesinger:

[1] *New York Times* Magazine, March 4, 1956.

The liberal, old style, or new style, swears by the evangels of Progress; he thinks of society as a machine for attaining material aggrandizement, and of happiness as the gratification of mundane desires.

Mr. Schlesinger rejoins by creating a highly stylized "conservative":

The conservative, on balance, opposes efforts at purposeful change because he believes that things are about as good as they can reasonably be expected to be, and that any change is more likely than not to be for the worse.

This judgment Mr. Kirk specifically rejects when he says: "The intelligent conservative does not set his face against all reform. Prudent social change is the means for renewing a society's vitality. . . ." The boys have a zestful time, however, laying about them with wooden swords.

Much of the quarreling between rival ideologies takes this general form. The socialist erects a horrid verbal image of a bloated capitalist and knocks it over with a bang, while the rugged individualist gleefully annihilates a stuffed and bearded figure which has practically nothing in common with, say, Mr. Norman Thomas.

Another form, common among strong-minded characters, is to generalize that what is good for oneself is good for everybody. My father, for instance, liked his soup excessively hot, and was positive that everybody followed his taste. He was severe with cooks who did not serve liquids at a scalding temperature, and refused to believe that plenty of us lacked his copper lining. Whatever holiday he planned was sure, he thought, to be extravagantly enjoyed by the rest of the family —or indeed by any family—and he brushed aside as incomprehensible all alternate suggestions.

Finally, there are the prophets and predictors who use the thin-entering-wedge argument, known in scientific circles as extrapolation. You take a case or two, propound a universal pattern therefrom, and project the curve into the future. The next chapter will be devoted to this fallacy.

OUR OLD CAT AND ANOTHER ONE

When I was about ten my grandfather once caught me indulging in a high, wide, and handsome generalization. He proceeded to tell me the story of our old cat, a story I have never forgotten.

A boy says: "Gee, there were a million cats in our back yard last night!"

"Did you count them?" asks his mother.

"No, but the place was full of cats."

"How many did you actually see?"

"Well, er, there was our old cat and another one."

My grandfather may not have cured me but he slowed me down.

A good deal of over-generalizing is harmless small talk. One weekend it rains, and the next weekend it rains again. So the suburban golf-players and gardeners assure each other that it "always rains on weekends."

It is only a step, however, to something much more dangerous. In Arizona I met a woman who said. "I've had to let Maria go, and I'll never hire another Mexican. You can't trust any of them, not one!" I tried to reason with her but she was too angry to listen. She was building up, you see, a formidable case of race prejudice based on one or two examples. Because a certain Mexican maid had disappointed her, she was condemning all Mexicans in one sweeping conclusion.

How much of the prejudice against Negroes, Yankees, Jews, Japanese, Britishers, Puerto Ricans, is similarly built up? One or two unfortunate experiences are developed into an ironclad rule rejecting a whole race, culture, or religious group. To make it worse, the rejector himself is often to blame for the unfortunate experiences through his failure to understand people of a different culture. How much of the conflict and misery and persecution in the world today arises from this kind of over-generalizing?

Here is Mr. Smith, of Middletown, Nebraska, who spends three days in Greece on a package tour. On his return, he gives a talk at the Thursday Club to tell his friends all about Greece. The modern Greeks, he says, are very backward people—they have no decent traffic lights, they spend all day drinking coffee in sidewalk cafés, and don't properly repair the Parthenon. Meanwhile Mr. Parnassos of Athens spends three days in Chicago on a package tour and returns to inform his friends in the sidewalk café that Americans spend their time killing each other with sawed-off shotguns when they are not being annihilated on the highways.

"When I am told," said Dean Acheson, "that Americans are idealistic, or that Frenchmen are logical, or Germans emotionally unstable, or Asians inscrutable, I always listen to the ensuing observation with skepticism. Not that such generalizations may not have some basis in fact, but they can rarely carry the superstructure erected on them."[2] After Pearl Harbor, the superstructure erected by Americans to describe the Japanese people was largely unprintable, with "little yellow monkeys" among the milder epithets. Today, the superstructure has shifted back approximately to where it was before the war. The Japanese people have probably not changed much, but American generalizations about them have undergone two violent shifts in a dozen years.

Chester Bowles in *Ambassador's Report* observes that after three months in India it would have been easy to write the book, for he had learned all the pat answers by that time.

[2] In *Harper's Magazine*, November, 1955.

After eighteen months it was much harder, for by then he knew that most of the pat answers were wrong. The longer he stayed, the more complicated India became. Messrs. Cohn and Schine, lieutenants of Senator McCarthy, were bothered by no such problem when they breezed through Europe in a few days, uncovering Communist conspiracies or evidence of "disloyalty" in various cities.

I KNOW A MAN WHO

Here is a group discussing social security after dinner. Mr. A. says: "I know a man who had eighteen thousand dollars in currency under his mattress, yet he went right ahead drawing benefits. That's social security for you!" A brisk battle then takes place on free enterprise versus the welfare state, with each contestant generalizing from a few hand-picked cases. "Would you hand the manufacture of atomic bombs over to Wall Street?" is countered by: "Would you hand the steel industry over to those bureaucrats in Washington?" Actually, of course, the U.S. Government must control certain activities in the public interest, such as atomic energy, while others are much better handled by private business. A meaningful discussion would attempt to find out where the line should be drawn.

At another dinner party I heard a woman say: "I had to take Leonard out of high school. Public schools are just impossible!" A man snaps back: "I'll never let John leave our high school. Private schools make children snobbish and they have no place in a democracy." Off they go for twenty minutes, while your author, sitting between the gunplay, has no chance to point out that it depends on the boy, the school, the teachers, the community, and quite a number of other things.

A politician in Rhode Island denounces compulsory automobile insurance. "It hasn't worked in Massachusetts," he thunders, "and it'll never work anywhere!"

At a public hearing in our town on two-acre zoning, a citizen arose and said he had heard that an acre of land had just been sold for two thousand dollars. "Now if this regulation goes through, and a young couple wants to build a house here, they will have to pay four thousand dollars for their land, and they simply can't afford it. What kind of democracy do you call that?" He sits down amid loud applause from the opposition. But there is still land in town to be had for two hundred dollars an acre. So an equally logical case could be made for a young couple starting life on a plot costing only four hundred dollars. Neither figure, of course, makes sense, for they are at the extreme ends of the cost spectrum. The real issue is a land cost somewhere in the middle, and, far more important for the young people's budget, the ratio of the land cost to the cost of the house.

Over the radio comes a news story of an escaped convict holding up a man and his wife in their home. He gets in the door on the plea that his car has broken down and he needs help. "That just goes to show," says a radio listener, "you don't dare help anyone in trouble any more!" If the whole community subscribed to this generalization, nobody would trust anybody, nobody would help anybody, and society would dissolve into anarchy. (Yes, this is a thumping generalization, too, but I believe that the assumption warrants the deduction.)

"Are you going to buy some of that new Ford stock, Mrs. Rowe?"

"No, I wouldn't touch it. Stocks are too risky!"

"What makes you think that?"

"Richard and I got caught in that Radio Common. It went down and down. It taught us a lesson, I can tell you!"

A valuable lesson, no doubt, but hardly enough to warrant avoiding the market all one's life. *What stocks, when, under what conditions, and recommended by whom?* Careful answers to these questions have returned some investors to the market after the debacle of the 1930's, to their considerable advantage.

IN A NUTSHELL

Headline writers are forced to over-simplify ideas as well as pick the shortest words. WORST DEFEAT SINCE CHINA turns out to be a gain by Communists in the Indonesian elections. Many of us are pretty well conditioned to discount the headlines. Before making up our minds we read the news story under them. In this case the story says that the Indonesian elections might, under certain circumstances, some day, prove to be a serious defeat for the West. People who read only headlines must receive a fantastically twisted picture of the current world.

The distortion is made worse by the readers' appetite for violence and conflict. An ugly strike is always news, but a peaceful settlement is something for the bottom of page 42. Newspaper readers, if they believe what is printed, tend to generalize a society abounding in murderers, kidnapers, rapists, abortionists, stick-ups, arson, riots, and car crashes.

It is a pleasure to announce, accordingly, that nine radio and television stations in Chicago have agreed on a joint program for reporting race disturbances in the lowest possible key, without inflammatory statements.[3] These stations promise not to use superlatives or adjectives which might "incite or enlarge a conflict." They will avoid the use of the word "riot" until the trouble has become serious enough to warrant it. They will carefully verify first reports and get the true facts

[3] *New York Times*, September 24, 1955.

before breaking a story. "Stories must be written in calm, matter-of-fact sentences, and in such a tone that they will not be inflammatory."

Commentators and columnists who daily interpret the news are under almost as much compulsion as headline writers. When trouble broke out in the Formosa Straits in 1954, its causes were very far from simple. Not only the two Chinas and the U.S. were involved, but Russia, Japan, Britain, France, India, and indeed all of Asia. But at 7 p.m., Eastern Standard Time, Walter Newcomb,[4] the globe-trotting expert, is forced to say: "Let's get this Formosa business down to brass tacks" —and does so in ninety seconds flat. Marquand gives us a commentary on some commentators as they operated in World War II:

Well, there you had it in a nutshell, or in a thumbnail sketch, if you want to put it that way. . . . The main thing is to remember that Hitler's timetable has been upset, and time was of the essence of gangster nations. . . . Jeffry knew that the picture which Walter gave of the war and soldiers was distorted. It was not fair to select such simplicity to illustrate something which was immense and tragic. . . . It would have been better if people like Walter would stay at home where they belonged instead of trying to round out pictures in a nutshell.

As an occasional writer for popular magazines I am aware of this nutshell trouble. Editors prefer a package neatly wrapped, with no ifs, ands, or buts. Qualifications slow the story and annoy readers, who want clean-cut dramatic unity and easy answers. But one cannot write honestly about modern political or social questions—say, the farm problem—without considerable qualification. Simplification can easily turn into distortion. Better not to write the article at all.

[4] Borrowing the name of a character in *So Little Time*, by John P. Marquand.

SOMEBODY ALWAYS GETS HURT

Arguments about a proposed law—a new tariff act, for instance—are nearly always corrupted by over-generalizing. Any major enactment is bound to hurt somebody, and the real issue is to strike a balance between gains and losses. Lower tariffs may hurt the wool business, but does the consumer gain enough to compensate? Such accounting takes time and thought. How much simpler for the wool manufacturers to cry havoc, the nation is ruined; and for importers of woolens to cry that prosperity will now advance to new peaks! What's good for General Motors may or may not be good for the country; the CIO publicity department is smarter with their slogan that what's good for the country is good for the CIO— but this might not always follow either.

Questions like these require thought and analysis, and many of them turn out like the story of the man who went down the street smashing windows. He said it was "good for trade." It might be good for the glass trade, but not for the store-keepers, while the waste made the whole community poorer.

IN SUMMARY

Why do we over-generalize so often and sometimes so disastrously? One reason is that the human mind is a generalizing machine. We would not be men without this power. The old academic crack: "All generalizations are false, including this one," is only a play on words. We *must* generalize to communicate and to live. But we should beware of beating the gun; of not waiting until enough facts are in to say something useful. Meanwhile it is a plain waste of time to listen to arguments based on a few hand-picked examples.

The generalizations we make are built up from cases the way a house is built out of stones, bricks, and lumber. If we see masons fitting large stones into a foundation, we are not likely to say: "This is going to be a stone house." If we see bricklayers starting a chimney we will hardly generalize: "This will be a brick house." In watching such physical operations, we have learned to wait until enough material is in place to warrant a reasonable inference about the kind of house it is going to be.

Chester Bowles did this about India. He waited until a great many facts were in place before telling us about that complicated country. But Chester Bowles, like the rest of us, if not on guard, could doubtless make two cats into a world of cats; two drunks into a reeling town, one swallow into a summer.

Generalizing is at the head of the reasoning process, and appears in many homely practices. Comparing, classifying, sorting, making bundles of similar objects and ideas, take up a substantial part of every normal person's day. The learning of children is largely generalizing—about doors, cars, dogs, slippery sidewalks; about spelling, arithmetic, and table manners. We also start new generalizations when we begin a collection of any kind—hi-fi records, stamps, autographs, prints. Much of this book is an exercise in generalizing about logical fallacies.

Generalizing is indeed central in the study of logic and the syllogism. Say the Liebers:[5]

A proposition may be *universal* (if it applies to all members of a class, like "All metals are elements"), or it may be *particular* (if it applies only to *some* members of a class, like "Some men are untrustworthy").

A person well grounded in logic is likely to be pretty shy of over-generalizing.

The story runs that a foreman took an intensive course

[5] *Mits, Wits and Logic.*

in human relations given by one of the universities and paid for by his company. It included careful fact finding and delayed decisions. "What are we going to do for exercise," he demanded, "now that we've stopped jumping to conclusions?"

In serious discussion and problem solving, I am afraid we shall have to give up that particular form of exercise, exhilarating as it may be. George Eliot phrases it well in *Middlemarch*: "This power of generalizing, which gives man so much the superiority in mistake over dumb animals."

6

Thin Entering Wedge

Fallacy Number Two

THE OVER-GENERALIZING described in the last chapter deals with events in the present and a few in the past. In this chapter we will concentrate on riding a curve into the future, predicting large, roomy conclusions on small scraps of fact. The thin-entering-wedge argument is also nicknamed the "camel's-nose-under-the-tent," and "give-them-an-inch-and-they'll-take-an-ell."

A good many of our arguments take the form:

If the U.S. tries to coexist with Russia, Communism will sweep the earth.

If we grant this union demand, the wage-price inflation spiral will wreck our economy.

If automation comes there will soon be twenty million unemployed.

If we let them get away with that exception it will be the end of zoning in this town.

If more hydrogen test bombs are exploded, the fall-out will ultimately destroy the race.

Or, to generalize these generalizations: If you do not do what I think ought to be done, disaster will surely follow.

It is easy to see the persuasiveness in this kind of argument. By pushing one's case to the limit, just short of an obvious *reductio ad absurdum*, one forces the opposition into a weaker position. The whole future is lined up against him. **Driven** to the defensive, he finds it hard to disprove something which has not yet happened.

Extrapolation is what scientists call such predictions, with the warning that they must be used with caution. A homely illustration is the driver who found three gas stations per mile along a stretch of the Montreal highway in Vermont, and concluded that there must be plenty of gas all the way to the North Pole. You chart two or three points, draw a curve through them, and then extend it indefinitely.

GREAT DEBATES

It is instructive to look back on various debates which once shook the country and compare the predictions, pro and con, with what actually happened after the issue was decided. As a young man I campaigned enthusiastically for woman's suffrage, making my first public speeches on Boston street corners. I said it would purify politics, end the rule of corrupt bosses, get the cigar smoke out of smoke-filled rooms, elect the best men, improve the public schools and public health, clean up the slums. My opponents on the soapbox were equally confident that the vote would destroy feminine charm, put women into trousers, reduce the birth rate, break up the home, and cause our forefathers, who said nothing about it in the Constitution, to turn in their graves.

Well, women got the vote in 1920 and what happened? Very little. The electorate was doubled with hardly any change in results; the Republic neither tottered nor reached the millennium. Few citizens now doubt that it is only fair and reasonable for women to have the right to vote. But my prediction of purified politics was as shaky as my opponents' vision of twenty-five million broken homes.

Where are the once fiery arguments about change after change which the American culture has since absorbed—the income tax, billion-dollar corporations, recognition of labor unions, conservation of natural resources, social security? Mostly gone with the wind. Those that are still around have largely lost their fire.

We were once solemnly assured that child labor couldn't be regulated without regulating all labor; minimum wages couldn't be fixed without fixing all wages; public housing couldn't be built unless the government built all housing. Some of us remember being promised from a score of platforms that proportional representation was the answer to all democracy's ills. The TVA, we were told, would usher in the complete monopoly of public power. Per contra, friends of the TVA, alarmed by a contract for a private plant in the area, reversed the argument by predicting that the Dixon-Yates deal marked the end of the TVA.

The National Association of Real Estate Boards still looks with alarm at public housing. A recent news letter leads off with this dire prediction:

Tyranny always begins by speaking in a soft voice and by explaining it only desires the good of the individual and the community. Every tyrant is self-righteous. Old Sam Johnson said 150 years ago, "There are few minds to which tyranny is not delightful.". . . We must stop public housing now so that it will not grow into an octopus which absorbs the whole housing industry. . . .

Instead of a camel's nose we have here the tentacle of an octopus, conceivably a better metaphor. It is doubtful if old Sam Johnson was thinking about public housing when he delivered that somewhat ambiguous line. Indeed, it is a bit puzzling to know *what* old Sam was referring to. If most minds find tyranny delightful, how did political democracy ever gather supporters?

Another current argument concerns the public schools. Everyone admits that there are not enough classrooms, teachers, or equipment. But at this point one faction demands federal aid which will solve everything, while another faction predicts that money from Washington will mean complete control of the curriculum by bureaucrats and politicians. This, the anti-federal-aiders imply, would be worse than no schools at all.

There are of course various safeguards which can be adopted to prevent federal control of education, following the safeguards whereby some local towns are protected from state control in receiving state aid. Sooner or later, one suspects, such safeguards will be applied, federal aid to schools will be granted, and the conflict will evaporate. In the meantime, unfortunately, a lot of children are going to suffer unnecessarily because of thin-entering-wedge logic, just as many children suffered because of the lag in the child labor law.

LETTERS TO THE EDITOR

Letters to the newspapers provide a gold mine of logical fallacies, especially dire predictions of the camel-octopus order. Here are a few, all appearing in New York journals in 1955.

A Brooklyn man notes that the steelworkers union has negotiated a wage increase. Whatever the pleasure for steelworkers, he says, it takes all the joy out of life for him. "As each new round of increases triggers general rises everywhere else, the fixed income groups are driven ever lower on the income scale. The dollar is cheapened, creditors and insurance policy owners lose. Where will it all end?" In ruin, obviously. But before joining the Brooklyn man in a good cry, we should remember that it *could* end in a cost of living held stationary, as increases in production per man hour offset increases in wages. At least that is what seems to have been actually happening since 1953.

Here is a lady, obviously very conservative in her views, and gravely distressed. She says the two-party system has ceased to function, for the Eisenhower Republicans are just as radical as the Democrats. She and her political friends are thus in effect disfranchised. "Allow the liberals to name both Presidential candidates in 1956," she warns, "and in our lifetime, we will see America stripped of defense against dictatorship and tyranny."

A New Jersey gentleman is deeply disturbed by American foreign policy. He is afraid that we are being disarmed by Russian smiles, and by Moscow's hospitality to visiting U.S. Senators. This is in effect collaboration, he says, and dangerous in the extreme. It will bring domination by the Kremlin. Anyone who favors it is a collaborator, he says, and such a person is "through with capitalism, through with Christianity, and through with America."

Many letters to the papers deal with juvenile delinquency and teen-agers, in pretty violent terms. One says: "We pamper our brats, gratifying every wish and whim. Result: they blossom into callous criminals who scoff at religion and morality." The gentleman is apparently handier with the rod than with the metaphor, for blossoming criminals are not seen every day.

A woman writer is also distressed about our pampered youngsters. "Our educational 'experts,' " she says, "are determined to hand our youth success on a silver platter!" They will grow soft and demoralized as a result, she says, without "guts or grit." The dear lady should start her trend curve a few years earlier. She seems to have forgotten the performance of our pampered young men in the late war. It took some guts and grit to storm the beach at Iwo Jima.

Here by contrast is a letter writer in *Time,* who chides the magazine for a piece of extrapolation. *Time,* he says, predicts that the loss of Quemoy to the Reds will mean the loss of Formosa, and mean the loss of all Asia. Lose one small island,

and a continent is gone, according to *Time*. "I have much more faith," says the correspondent, "in our Seventh Fleet."

An oil man from Texas writes a bristling letter to the *New York Times* advocating the passage of the natural gas bill, which would relieve the industry of federal regulation. He is furious at the Supreme Court for upholding such regulation in an earlier decision. "One of the shames of this political crime," he says, "is that it brings into being the first act of governmental regulation of all businesses and the overthrow of free enterprise. . . ."

Letters such as these can be multiplied indefinitely. The writer begins with a grievance, often a legitimate one. But rather than considering it in relation to other current problems, and especially in relation to a similar problem in the past, he rushes headlong into the future until his grievance fills the sky. Mr. A. sees a wild inflation destroying the economy. Mrs. B. sees America subverted by liberals and ripe for a dictator. Mr. C. sees "coexistence" as the finish of capitalism and Christianity. Mr. D. sees the younger generation "blossoming" into criminals, while Miss E. sees it going soft, without grit or guts. Mr. F. envisions a Supreme Court decision as the end of free enterprise.

Senator Carl Hayden of Arizona is also pretty annoyed at the courts for holding up the printing of one of his reports. Said he in a prepared statement in May, 1956:

If a court can enjoin Congress from issuing a report it will be only a matter of time before our remarks on the floor of the Senate . . . would be subject to a judicial review, and a complete breakdown of the constitutional principle of separation of powers would ensue.

CRISIS IN THE MORNING

Extrapolation is by no means confined to large political issues. You wake in the morning, let us say, with an unaccustomed pain somewhere in your interior. Your mind proceeds to expand this sensation into a future of the gloomiest nature. You lie there imagining a grim sequence of medical examinations, X-rays, hospitals, leading all too soon to the grave. An hour or two later, after your second cup of coffee, the pain has vanished and with it the extrapolation. A little understanding of the mechanism enables us to correct these soaring curves which seem to doom our health, or our family relationships, or our solvency.

Scientists often use extrapolation to discover the future, with very fruitful results, *but only when they have nailed down enough points to warrant the curve.* We should try to follow this course, both in our personal and political judgments. If the pain comes three mornings in a row and persists, we had better see a doctor. If a formidable array of facts indicates that the Chinese Reds are going to use the capture of Quemoy as a steppingstone to the invasion of Formosa, the U.S. position in Asia may very well be imperiled.

Thin entering wedges can and do split great rocks. But the process is not inevitable for all rocks, or for all types of wedges.

7

Getting Personal

Fallacy Number Three

> **AD HOMINEM**

THE CLASSIC example of this fallacy is a scene in a British court of law. As the attorney for the defense takes the floor, his partner hands him a note: "No case. Abuse the plaintiff's attorney."

If you can't shake the argument, abuse the person who advances it, and so discredit it through the back door. Go from facing the issue, which jurists call *ad rem,* to the man, *ad hominem.*

A story is told about Lincoln as a young lawyer.[1] In one of his first jury cases, he showed his political shrewdness by an adroit and quite non-malicious use of *ad hominem.* His opponent was an experienced trial lawyer, who also had most of the fine legal points on his side. The day was warm and Lincoln slumped in his chair as the case went against him. When the orator took off his coat and vest, however, Lincoln sat up with a gleam in his eye. His opponent was wearing one of the new city-slicker shirts of the 1840's, which buttoned up the back.

Lincoln knew the reactions of frontiersmen, who made up the jury. When his turn came, his plea was brief: "Gentlemen of the jury, because I have justice on my side, I am sure you

[1] Mary Alkus in *Coronet,* September, 1953.

will not be influenced by this gentleman's pretended knowledge of the law. Why, he doesn't even know which side of
his shirt ought to be in front!"

Lincoln's *ad hominem* is said to have won the case.

This fallacy, like over-generalizing, has been around for a
long time. The Sophists must have used it freely, and I suspect
it goes back to the dawn of the race.

First cave man: "Heard the latest on old man Fist Ax? He's
putting feathers on his arrows. Says they go straighter."

Second cave man: "Forget it. Nobody who's such a wife-
stealer could come up with a decent idea."

Not every personal attack, however, can be classed as
faulty logic. When the scandal of Grover Cleveland's illegitimate son was used against him in the presidential campaign,
the argument had some point. Did Americans want a President of such a character? (The sovereign voters decided that
his virtues overrode his defects.) If, however, Cleveland's
enemies had introduced the natural son as an argument against
his tariff policy, then a true *ad hominem* would appear. In the
first case, Cleveland himself was the issue; in the second the
tariff was the issue. When a man is running for office, or being
chosen for any position in government or elsewhere, his personal behavior is always relevant. A corporation would naturally hesitate to hire as treasurer a man who had been
convicted of embezzlement.

The health of President Eisenhower was an important con-
sideration in the nominations of 1956. Was he well enough
to serve out another four years in the toughest job in the
world? Similarly with Franklin Roosevelt in 1944. But when
the enemies of Roosevelt charged that a given government
policy was wrong because it originated with "that cripple in
the White House," they were practicing a particularly vicious
kind of *ad hominem*.

IF THE PREMISES ARE SUFFICIENT

"If the premises are sufficient," said Morris R. Cohen, "they are so no matter by whom stated." A person's unreliable character may weaken his credibility as a witness when reporting what he himself has observed. But in an objective argument his character, and even his motives, should be ignored.

Cohen cites a number of examples. When an attempt was made to refute Spinoza's views on the nature of matter because he had renounced Judaism, lived alone, and was considered queer, we have a pure case of *ad hominem*. Galileo's theory of the tides was independent of his motives in advancing it. The peccadillos of Gauss as a young man had nothing to do with the validity of his proof that every equation has a root. "The evidences for a physical theory are in the physical facts relevant to it, and not in the personal motives which led anyone to take an interest in such questions."

The theory of evolution developed by Darwin and Huxley a century ago demonstrated, among other things, that the biblical date of creation, 4004 B.C., as worked out by Bishop Usher, was too recent. The world was a good deal older than that. Not thousands but millions of years were needed to evolve the various species we know today. Many religious people were shocked, among them Bishop Wilberforce. In a famous public debate he asked Huxley with suitable irony: "Are you descended from a monkey on your mother's side or on your father's?"

The *ad hominem* of course brought down the house. The worthy bishop evaded the scientific issue by resorting to a wise-crack about Huxley's family tree. In the 1860's this seemed the height of wit and wisdom. Today it sounds remarkably silly.

ARE YOU A TECHNOCRAT?

Some years ago I was asked by a committee of citizens to testify in a legal action in a nearby Connecticut city. I had recently made a study of population trends in the U.S., and the committee wanted me to apply the formulas to forecast the growth of the city. The legal case concerned a new private reservoir for the municipal water supply. I presented a careful report, with a number of charts and tables, and when I finished the lawyer for the other side began his cross-examination by questioning my figures. This was right and proper. Finding no serious discrepancies there, he shuffled his notes, took a step in my direction, looked me sternly in the eye, and demanded: "Mr. Chase, were you ever a Technocrat?"

Though this had no connection with the future population of western Connecticut, I saw that it was intended to discredit me as an expert witness. (Today, of course he would have asked me if I had ever belonged to any organization on the Attorney General's list.) Technocrats were then popularly supposed to be crackpots, incapable of giving reliable figures. I looked him back in the eye and said that I had never been a Technocrat. At the height of the craze, I said, I had written a pamphlet about Technocracy, containing several severe criticisms. If learned counsel would like to see a copy, I said, I could probably find one in my files.

That was the end of that; I managed to counter the *ad hominem*. Many other witnesses in recent years have not been so fortunate.

Moving to a broader political level, we recall the attacks on Dean Acheson during his last year as Secretary of State. Any policy or proposal of his, or of his department, was denounced as the height of folly, if not worse, by many citizens, led by the majority of the nation's newspapers. Some of

Acheson's proposals were excellent, some not, but the critics did not look at the proposals. They looked only at the man who sponsored them. By temporarily discrediting the man, they effectively weakened and confused the foreign policy of the United States. Any top politician runs this risk; it may await the present Secretary.

"POISONING THE WELL"

Another name for the *ad hominem* fallacy is "poisoning the well." In recent years, the poison has been applied to books, paintings, works of art, in the great Communist spy hunt here in America. The hunters did not open the books or inspect the paintings; enough that they were the work of somebody who had been accused by somebody of being soft toward Communism. Thus *The Thin Man,* an excellent detective story, was forced off the shelves of libraries maintained by the State Department overseas, because its author had plead the Fifth Amendment before a Congressional Committee. The same book, word for word, written by an author *not* involved with the Committee would not have been censored, for it had no political implications.

This kind of censorship became so common at one time that it received the special name "book-burning." President Eisenhower assailed the book-burners in a forthright speech at Dartmouth College. Any book by an author who had ever been charged with subversive ideas—or indeed with having any ideas at all—was likely to be hidden under the counter, or thrown out altogether.

An official censor in Memphis, Tennessee, forbade the showing of an ancient film by Charlie Chaplin, a satire on Carmen. The censor threatened to send the police if it was exhibited at the First Unitarian Church as advertised. Chaplin was then under a loyalty cloud, but not *Carmen.* The church called off the public showing as ordered, but a private showing was staged before the church trustees, who of course could find nothing subversive in *Carmen.* So the Rev. Richard Gibbs, pastor of the church, exhibited the film to the public at the next regular meeting, saying: "We feel that a principle is at stake here, whether a group of mature people shall be told what is morally fit for them to be associated with in their church life."

In 1956 the Museum of Fine Arts in Dallas undertook to exhibit "Sport in Art," a series of paintings by celebrated artists, collected by *Sports Illustrated.* The Dallas County Patriotic Council attacked the exhibit, saying that four of the artists had once been members of so-called Communist-front groups. The Council said that art is used by Communists to "brainwash and create public attitudes that are soft toward Communism." The four paintings at issue showed, respectively, a winter scene, a baseball game, an elderly fisherman, and a group of skaters. It is pleasant to report that the trustees of the Art Museum supported their right to exhibit the paintings, and denounced the Patriotic Council's intervention. The *New York Times* said editorially, on May 27, 1956: "The Dallas Museum permitted the pictures to be shown without, so far as we can tell, creating a single new Communist vote in Dallas County."

IN REVERSE

Senator Wayne Morse provides us with a case from the other side of the fence. When the Senate was considering the funds for various investigating committees, the Senator was bombarded with telegrams and long-distance telephone calls from liberals, urging him to vote against the appropriations. Why? Because of the record of the men who headed the committees. "They wanted me to assume," said Morse, "that the appropriations would be misspent. . . . I resented this because these people were dealing in *ad hominem* attacks."

Senator Morse did not approve of the tactics of certain com-

mittee chairmen any more than did the telegram writers, but
he saw the real issue far more clearly. The real issue was the
power of the Senate to investigate, not the character of the
men who, from time to time, depending on the party in
power, and on seniority, might chair the committees.

Ad hominem is used by liberals as well as conservatives,
and is likely to be used by anyone who wants to put over a
fast argument, or save himself the mental effort of examining
a given issue. We have all heard the complaint that Smith's
ideas for the new high school cannot be any good because
Smith never got a degree. So we need spend no time studying
his plan. We all know the father who laughs off his young
son's explanation why the family car coughs like a wounded
gorilla. The idea must be worthless, the father thinks, because
Junior is still so very junior—he never picks up his things.
But Junior, like thousands of American boys, may have such
a passion for internal-combustion engines that he understands
their various indispositions—and this is the real issue.

Once grasped, *ad hominem* is easy to identify—in oneself as
well as in others. Presently we find it snarling up radio discussion programs, news stories, editorials, political speeches—
especially political speeches. Is the speaker sticking to the issue
or is he attacking the character of somebody who defends the
issue? Because most of us tend to think more in terms of
personalities than of issues, *ad hominem* is often very tempt-
ing. But, like Ulysses, we must resist the siren call.

In the prologue to *Fanny's First Play*, Bernard Shaw pre-
sents a drama critic who, after a private showing, complains
that the playwright's name has been withheld. "How can I
tell whether it's a good play," he demands, "unless I know who
wrote it?"

8

"You're Another"

Fallacy Number Four

**TU
QUOQUE**

I**F THE** typical example of *ad hominem* is in a British court,
that of *tu quoque* is in a Russian subway.

The story runs that when the Moscow underground was
first opened to visitors in the 1930's, an American tourist was
invited to inspect one of the stations. He was shown the self-
registering turnstiles and the spotless washrooms. "Fine," he
said; then, looking down the tracks, "How about the trains?"
They showed him the safety devices and the excellent tile
frescos on the tunnel walls. He was again impressed, but continued to look anxiously down the tracks.

"How about the trains?" snapped his guide. "How about
the trains? How about the sharecroppers in Alabama?"

Tu quoque, literally translated, means "Thou also," and
in the vernacular, "You're another!" The Oxford dictionary
defines it as "an argument which consists of rotating a charge
upon one's accuser." Instead of speaking to the issue, one
launches an irrelevant counterattack. In algebra, a minus
multiplied by a minus makes a plus, but in straight thinking
two wrongs do not make a right.

John Gunther in *Inside Africa* relates how he was upbraided
by European residents for the mistreatment of American

Indians in U.S. history. "Look," they said, "you exterminated your natives, but we try to educate our blacks." This, they thought, was a complete answer to any criticism by Americans of discrimination against native Africans.

Here again two wrongs do not make a right. Says Gunther: "The fact that Americans have behaved abominably toward Indians does not excuse Europeans of the present day for doing the same." The American Indians who survived, furthermore, have a higher legal and social status than Negroes in South Africa. Intermarriage is not looked down on in most sections of America. A prominent New York lawyer of my acquaintance never loses a chance to boast that one of his ancestors was a full-blooded Indian. There is no real parallel between the case of red Indians and black Africans, for in America the whites were soon in the majority, while in Africa they are still far in the minority.

Zoning, which as a hot local issue in our town seems to provide me with a number of cases, offers an excellent example of this fallacy too. A resident was denied permission to break open a new door in his stone garage, giving directly on the road some eight feet away. The Board of Appeals found a serious traffic hazard in backing a car out of the proposed opening. The owner indignantly protested. "Why," he said, "my door wouldn't be nearly as bad a traffic hazard as the cars I see parked in front of houses all over town!" Even if what he said was true, it was beside the point. The point was that zoning decisions are supposed to prevent *additional* traffic hazards.

A man comes home from a January clothing sale with a sport jacket which is practically self-illuminating. Proudly he tries it on, only to hear his wife say: "My dear, how loud! Couldn't you find something a little quieter?"

"Well, you get yourself up in some pretty noisy numbers, and not any too becoming either!"

And off they go in a family row, fed by new and old grievances, rather than sticking to the legitimate issue. Instead of firing a *tu quoque*, the man might have quoted the salesman to the effect that loud plaids were all the rage this year, and the jacket would put him on a level with the North Shore set. An appeal to fashion might well have mollified his wife, and the couple could have had an amiable discussion on blistering plaids and current styles.

Bennett Cerf once complained, in his column in the *Saturday Review*, that a standard box lunch cost $1.50 at the San Francisco airport, and only $1.00 at Eastern airports. Peppery letters from the West Coast were soon in the mails. Go down in the New York subway, said one, and pay six cents for a five-cent candy bar. Put a dime in a New York stamp machine and get only eight cents' worth of stamps; out here, said the letter writer, we get nine cents' worth. Pay ninety-five cents for admission to "Do-it-yourself" shows in the East, and walk in free throughout the West.

All true, but the point still remains: Should the traveler pay $1.50 for a box lunch at San Francisco?

Revolving arguments of this type are common enough. Still more common is the standard one-two: "You're a liar!" "You're another!" Small boys in back lots, and larger boys in bars, make this retort as an automatic reflex, hardly to be dignified as logical. We note the reflex and pass on to matters where reason is at least supposed to operate.

POLITICAL GIVE-AND-TAKE

The chairman of the Republican National Committee and his opposite member on the Democratic National Committee engage in a kind of perpetual *tu quoque,* as formalized and stately as a seventeenth-century minuet. The Democratic chairman calls a press conference to announce that the Republican candidate is receiving a secret fund from large oil operators. Within an hour the Republican chairman has a release on the wires affirming that the Democratic candidate receives secret funds from the CIO.[1] A top party logician, giving a lecture to the faithful on answering campaign arguments, laid down the rule: "If he asks you where you stand on Dulles, jump right in and ask him where he stands on Acheson."

David Lawrence, a vigorous Republican of the Taft school, in his daily column often proves himself a master of *tu quoque*. When some unpleasantness develops in the Republican administration upon which the Democrats might happily capitalize, he directs his able research staff to find a parallel in past Democratic administrations. Thus when the Secretary for the Air Force, a Republican, was charged while in high office with advancing the interests of a private engineering firm, Mr. Lawrence reminded his readers that Franklin D. Roosevelt saw nothing amiss in allowing his private secretary, Louis Howe, to receive substantial sums for a weekly broadcast.[2] The cases were not quite parallel, but Mr. Lawrence equated them with skill.

Again, when the Senate Banking Committee, controlled by Democrats, criticized a prominent Republican administrator for overlooking the distinction between public duty and private business, Mr. Lawrence promptly pointed out how administrative boards had been packed by New Dealers not so many years ago, and how "the labor bosses defeated the confirmation of Judge John J. Parker for the Supreme Court because he had, in a matter of law, ruled against a labor union."

Sometimes below this perennial exchange of political rhetoric

[1] Cf. the Nixon and Stevenson battle of funds in 1952.
[2] New York *Herald Tribune,* July 27, 1955.

we strike a more sordid *tu quoque*. One party discovers a piece of personal scandal concerning a candidate of the other party and threatens to release it—reluctantly of course—as a duty to the country. The high command of the other party then beats the bushes for an offsetting item. In the 1940 presidential campaign, fast work by the Democrats, it is said, prevented the disclosure of a very warm piece of news in possession of the Republicans. The unpleasant details need not concern us here, but I heard them firsthand from one of the bush-beaters.

Mr. Dooley, the sage of Archie Road, noted *tu quoque* arguments inside the same political camp. "When ye see two men with white neckties go into a sthreet car an' set in opposite corners while one mutthers 'thraitor' an' th' other hisses 'miscreent,' ye can bet they're two dimmycratic leaders thryin' to reunite th' ol' party."

FOREIGN MATTER

Somebody writes a letter to the papers attacking Russian propaganda. Somebody else—not necessarily a fellow traveler —replies that it is no worse than U.S. propaganda threatening "massive retaliation." In the fracas, the techniques of Red propaganda, a very real issue today, are never objectively examined.[3]

Here is a letter to the *Times* saying in effect: "Who are we to complain about Red China's atrocities after what the U.S. did at Hiroshima?" Again one wrong is proffered to cancel another wrong—a specious logic frequently displayed in wartime propaganda.

When the Russian-drilled army of North Korea crossed the 38th Parallel to attack the South Koreans on June 25, 1950, the Communists of the world staged a *tu quoque* so massive

[3] As I shall try to do in Chapter 21.

that it can also be labeled a Big Lie. Day and night, beginning in 1950, year after year, the Reds continued to repeat that it was the *South Koreans* who first attacked the long-suffering North Koreans. Factual disproof, though ample, had little effect. For a time more than half the world may have believed this story, which completely reversed the actual situation, and millions, I suspect, still believe it.

Tu quoque becomes a logical fallacy only when it is used to avoid a real issue. We are not concerned with loud verbal exchanges on the eleven-year-old level of You're-a-liar-you're-another. The issue must be general and capable of intelligent discussion. These issues may range from fashions in sport jackets, to global trends. Politics, as noted, has many authentic issues which transcend campaign oratory. When these important matters are smothered in cries of "You're another," serious social and economic problems remain unsolved.

Tu quoque will normally be thrown out of any courtroom. Imagine the defendant arguing with the judge in a traffic case: "Sure I was drunk when I knocked him over, but he was drunk too!"

How about the trains; how about the trains? Well, how about them?

9

Cause and Effect

Fallacy Number Five

**POST HOC
ERGO
PROPTER
HOC**

CHANTECLER, the cock in Rostand's famous play, observed that after he crowed the sun came up. Therefore, he reasoned, his crowing caused the sun to rise. This illustrates perfectly what logicians call the *post hoc* fallacy. When one event precedes another event in time, the first is assumed to be the cause of the second.

Malaria was for centuries a baffling plague. It was observed that persons who went out at night often developed the malady. So, on the best *post hoc* reasoning, night air was assumed to be the cause of malaria, and elaborate precautions were taken to shut it out of sleeping quarters. Some scientists, however, were skeptical of this theory. A long series of experiments eventually proved that malaria was caused by the bite of the *anopheles* mosquito. Night air entered the picture only because mosquitoes prefer to attack in the dark.

As I write, two *post hoc* arguments are much in the news: the first, cigarette-smoking causes lung cancer; the second, test explosions of atomic bombs cause hurricanes and floods. Let us examine them.

More men are smoking cigarettes, and more men are de-

71

veloping lung cancer. Some careful statistical studies show a correlation. But many doctors are skeptical, saying that one or more other causes, such as polluted air, fumes, "smog," may contribute to the effect. We do not yet have enough facts to know whether this widely publicized reasoning is a fallacy or not. The logical thing to do in the circumstances is to defer our conclusions until the facts are in.[1]

Various sections of the globe, such as the northeast coast of the United States, have suffered from unaccustomed hurricanes and floods in recent years. The U.S. Armed Services meanwhile have been exploding atomic and hydrogen bombs, for experimental purposes, in Nevada and the Pacific. Therefore, the reasoning runs, the explosions cause the hurricanes by disturbing higher air currents. Most atomic scientists deny any connection. Furthermore, the worst New England hurricanes to date, those of 1938 and 1944, arrived before any atomic bombs had been exploded. *Newsweek* in July, 1954, ran the following story:

Red propagandists aren't missing any bets. Soviet and satellite radio broadcasts are blaming Europe's current floods on American H-bomb tests, which, they say, disturbed the atmosphere and caused heavy rains.

Now that the Russians themselves are exploding H-bombs, their enemies can return the compliment whenever the weather gets out of hand. My guess is that we have here a genuine *post hoc* fallacy; the test explosions have not yet upset the weather, except locally, whatever they might do to it in an all-out atomic war.

TO FILL AN EXPLANATORY VACUUM

The full Latin name for the fallacy is *Post hoc, ergo propter hoc*, which translates: "After this, therefore because of this."

[1] Facts are still coming in and increasingly seem to indicate a causal connection.

It is responsible for a large amount of misunderstanding and conflict. It operates on all levels, from the cucumbers which you are sure caused a stomach-ache, to the H-bombs which some people are sure cause hurricanes half a world away.

What *is* the cause of a given effect? Often it is obvious, as when a fall on the ice results in a sprained wrist. But often it is not at all obvious, as in the case of malaria. Many events result from not one cause but from a whole process. The stomach-ache may be due to cucumbers, plus too many martinis, plus an acrimonious argument at dinner, plus worry about a possible layoff at the office. Scientists, as mentioned earlier, increasingly think in terms of process, rather than simple cause and effect.

Post hoc reasoning helps us fill an explanatory vacuum. We do not like uncertainty, and if we can't find a reason for a given occurrence we feel baffled and unhappy. Any reason, even a flimsy one, seems better than no reason at all. John Dewey once explored this idea in *The Quest for Certainty*.

Frost comes. Leaves turn. Therefore frost turns the leaves. Few happenings in nature are more solidly accepted. But for certain years in southern Connecticut, I have observed glorious displays of autumn foliage *before* the first frost. Scientists say that frost has little to do with the process, which they attribute to chemical changes as sap recedes in the tree. Indeed a strict disciple of *post hoc* should reason, in the years when the leaves turn first, that autumn foliage induces frost.

IN THE JURY ROOM

Courts today are crowded with accident cases, and *post hoc* hovers over most of them. The jury must decide whether or not the current indispositions and misfortunes of the plaintiff are due to a prior accident. If they are, what is their dollar value? Medical testimony is often flatly contradictory, one expert arguing a *post hoc*, the other denying it. The jury has to battle its way through logic good and bad, trying to come to a just verdict; it has to imitate in a crude way what a scientist does in an exact way.

Here are two cases considered recently by a Connecticut jury on which my wife happened to serve. A girl receives a head injury in a motor accident. Subsequently she gets a job as receptionist for a doctor, but she does not hold it long. She sues the insurance company for damages, claiming that the accident prevents her from keeping her mind on her work. She thinks she is damaged about thirty thousand dollars' worth. Was the accident the cause of her incompetence? The jury is inclined to think the accident contributed, but not to the tune of thirty thousand dollars.

A real estate broker is injured by furniture falling on him in a house he is showing to a client. He sues the owner. He says he hasn't been well since the accident. Among other symptoms, he becomes very tired in the afternoon. The lawyer for the defense inquires how old the broker is, and remarks, with appropriate legal sarcasm: "I get tired in the afternoon too, and nothing has fallen on me except my age."

Serving on a jury, says my wife, gives excellent practice in avoiding the pitfalls of *post hoc* reasoning.

MEDICAL MATTERS

Natives of the New Hebrides in the South Pacific hold the unshakable conviction that lice keep a person healthy. They observe that practically all healthy natives have lice, while sick people often do not, ergo lice must be the cause of good health. The real explanation, however, is quite different. When a person falls sick in that tropical climate he usually runs a fever. Lice do not like it that hot and they leave.[2]

I was brought up to believe that wet feet produced colds,

[2] Darrell Huff, *How to Lie with Statistics*.

and was taught to take elaborate precautions against them. This reasoning was a *post hoc*, but not a pure one. Wet feet do not produce colds but may contribute to them indirectly by lowering the body's resistance. A person who keeps his blood circulating by exercise, says a lumberman, can have wet feet for days and not develop a cold. Here again a *process* is involved, not a simple cause and effect.

At a convention in San Francisco in the spring of 1955, someone reported from the platform that he had recently seen President Eisenhower, who did not look in the best of health. Instantly a delegate jumped up on the floor and cried: "Washington drinks fluoridated water; that's the trouble with Ike!" The fact that a million or so other Washingtonians were feeling reasonably well did not count.[3]

BLACK CATS

A woman sees a black cat and later in the day loses her pocketbook. The cat, she says, caused the loss. Most of us average some kind of misfortune every day of our lives, with a greater misfortune perhaps once a week. To reason that the sight of a black cat, or passing under a ladder, or spilling salt, causes these routine misfortunes is pure *post hoc*.

People continue to believe that if milk is left around in open pans, a clap of thunder will sour it. What actually happens is that thunderstorms usually come on hot days, and heat encourages the bacteria which cause milk to sour. Lightning and thunder have nothing to do with it.

Another celestial matter in which uncounted Americans still believe, if the ads are any indication, is astrology. You were born under such and such a sign, therefore all important experiences throughout your life can be laid to the position of the stars at your birth. It apparently pleases many people to

[3] The *Reporter*, June 30, 1955.

believe that the orbs of heaven watch over their fortunes. But
no scientific connection has ever been established; indeed no
operation to prove it could conceivably be set up. What *can*
happen, of course, is that a student of astrology may firmly
believe that he is lucky or unlucky, according to the chart.
Such belief may, to a degree impossible to determine, influence his behavior.

A strong team of Japanese mountain-climbers was given
permission by the native government to climb Manaslu, one
of the great peaks of the Himalayas. In 1954 the team arrived
in the village of Sama. More than four hundred porters, laden
with food and equipment, escorted them. The villagers attacked the party with sticks and stones so violently that the
porters dropped their loads and fled. Why the violence? A
nice case of *post hoc*. The villagers explained that "heathen
Japanese," scouting for the climb the year before, had dese-
crated their holy mountain. The gods had therefore loosed a
great avalanche, which destroyed a lamasery and killed three
priests. It was admitted that the avalanche came six months
after the visit of the exploring party, but no villager doubted
the connection.

Sometimes we try to influence future events by *post hoc*
reasoning, and a favorite subject among country-dwellers is
the weather. We joke about it of course, but are we not half
serious? "The garden," I say, "is drying up. I've done everything to make it rain—left out the tennis rackets, washed the
car, planned a picnic for Saturday with no cover anywhere
near the beach—everything. And not a drop!"

More grim were the *post hocs* of the ancient Aztecs. In
their experience rain had followed the season of sacrificial
rites, and they believed that sacrificing a human being with
due ceremony would make rain come again, and turn the

milpas green. Practically all sacrifices of men or animals down
the ages bear horrible testimony to the fallacy.

A good deal of modern advertising bears similar testimony,
but more fanciful than horrible. Copy often takes the form:

SHE IS ENGAGED! Picture of beautiful lady with dreamy expression.

SHE USES BLOTTO'S FACE POWDER. Picture of package.

THEREFORE, it is implied, if YOU use Blotto's face powder, YOU TOO
will become engaged.

Thus *post hoc* substantially aids copywriters dedicated to
capitalizing human longing. We do so want to be engaged,
or to have lovely teeth, or be the life of the party, or a man
of distinction.

SUNSPOTS AND STATISTICS

In 1875 the noted economist Jevons advanced the theory
that the business cycle was caused by sunpots. This had a
little more to it than Chantecler's theory, but not much more.
Even today, one economist seriously argues that the path of
the planet Venus, interrupting solar radiation, affects weather
and crops and causes eight-year cycles. Economists who value
their reputation are pretty shy of sunspots. The ups and downs
of business, they say, have many causes, especially the alterna-
tion of over-optimism and over-pessimism among businesmen,
depending in turn on the behavior of consumers.

After damn lies, in the old saying, come statistics. The
trouble in considering statistical *post hocs* is not so much with
the figures as with the conclusions drawn from them. In our
expanding economy, records of production, sales, and the like,
keep moving up year after year. The fallacy creeps in when
one upward-moving curve is said to be the *cause* of another.
In England, imports of bananas rose regularly for years, and
so did cases of tuberculosis. The figures were unimpeachable,

but the conclusion, widely heralded, that eating bananas caused TB was plain crazy. Figures show juvenile crime increasing in the U.S., and also sales of comic books. Now there *may* be a connection, but all we have to date is a rough clue.

Unless statistics like these are handled with asbestos gloves they will kindle *post hocs* in all directions. Huff cites another exhibit concerning cigarettes. Reliable figures demonstrate, he says, that college students who smoke them receive lower average grades than those who do not. The anti-nicotine reformers seize on these figures to "prove" that cigarettes lower scholarship. The figures could equally well "prove" the reverse, namely that low marks drive students not to drink, but to tobacco. The most probable reason, however, says Huff, is that the sociable type likes to smoke and does not want to be known as a grind—C-minus is good enough for him. There are several plausible explanations for the correlation between the two figures; we are not entitled to select the one that suits our case.

The number of college students per thousand of U.S. population is rising. So is the number of inmates in mental hospitals, so is the incidence of heart disease, output of false teeth, salaries of California schoolteachers, production of electric washing machines, left-handed batters struck out, and what have you. Take the first two curves above: college students and mental cases, both advancing. This "proves," does it not, that going to college is likely to unbalance the mind?

A fairly close statistical correlation can be worked out between the price of rum in Havana and the salaries of ministers in Massachusetts. Both are affected by the secular inflation of the last hundred years. There is no possible connection otherwise, but an embittered atheist might attempt to prove that Massachusetts ministers are using their increased salaries to buy more rum, or that the rum trade supports the ministry!

Deductions from statistics can fall into various classes of logical fallacies. Here we use examples to illustrate *post hoc* reasoning. In Chapter 12 we will select other statistical examples to illustrate the fallacy of *ad verecundiam*, appeal to authority. The latter includes reverence for figures as such, the curious notion, widely held especially in the U.S., that a string of decimal places can't be wrong.

IN SUMMARY

Post hoc logic is all around us, and will trip the wisest unless he is on guard. It is especially likely to trip us in three kinds of situation:

1. Something happens, and presently something else happens, with considerable regularity. It looks as if the first causes the second, but actually it does not. A cockcrow does not make the sun come up.

2. In an even more common form, event A *may* affect B, but in a minor way, as part of a process which includes other causes. Cucumbers may be one small item in a complicated process which brings on a pain in the stomach.

3. Events A and B move together in a time scale, but which is cart and which is horse? Or, as in the case of Havana rum and Massachusetts clergymen, are both due to a larger general cause? Or is there any connection at all?

Any parallel movement of two events, to be sure, can give us a *clue*. But as readers of detective stories well know, for one correct clue there are a dozen false ones. A hunch may be all right to start with; scientific discovery often begins with a hunch. But science and sound logic cannot stop there; they must go on collecting facts and weighing them until real proof can be demonstrated.

Here is a public official who seems to have done just this. New York City's Police Commissioner, Stephen P. Kennedy, surveys automobile fatalities for the first forty days of 1956.[4] Look, he says, they are 20 percent less than for the first forty days of 1955. Furthermore, he says, in 1956 we used police cars without special markings, but in 1955 they could be recognized as official cars. The stage is thus set for a ringing *post hoc*, and the newspaper headline does not disappoint us. *Because* police cars cruised amid the traffic unmarked, they apprehended more wild drivers and so kept fatalities down. Q.E.D.

But Commissioner Kennedy is apparently a student of logical fallacies. He declined to draw any conclusion from the seemingly related facts, holding that "the success of the new techniques cannot be judged in so short a time." What a paragon for all of us to follow!

[4] *New York Times*, February 13, 1956.

10

False Analogies

Fallacy Number Six

THE UNITED STATES is building a string of radar stations around the country, including installations in northern Canada. Writing to one of the New York papers in 1954, a man calls it wishful thinking to believe that a wall of radar across Canada can stop enemy bombers. "Look at the Great Wall of China," he says, "look at the Maginot Line." Having established his two analogies, he goes on to argue that the only defense against invaders is a preventive war; go out and hit them first!

There is no real comparison between the Great Wall of China, designed to hold against nomadic horsemen armed with spears, the Maginot Line, designed to repel mass infantry charges, and an electronic detector of bombing planes moving at the speed of sound. About all they have in common is the word "wall." On this shaky analogy, Mr. X. is willing to plunge the world into an atomic war.

On another level, analogies can be helpful. Here is a good one from Gilbert W. Chapman of the National Book Committee:

There is no reason to make either books or education easy, any more than tennis or football is easy. Like sport, they require a certain amount of hard work and practice, and like sport, they can be both a challenge and a delight.

We have all seen models of the atom, with its nucleus and revolving electrons. No one has ever seen an actual atom or possibly ever will. Models like this in physics, says Dr. Percy Bridgman, are useful tools of thought, picturing the unfamiliar in terms of the familiar. A working model is of course an analogy, a more precise one. In the laboratory model we multiply the theoretical dimensions by a factor large enough "to bring it to the magnitude of ordinary experience."

Bridgman's definition is applicable to analogies in general. Do they really fit the case? To compare radar stations in Canada with the Great Wall of China only befuddles the mind. No analogy, whether in physics, politics, or anywhere else, can conclusively prove anything. The best it can do is to help bring the event under discussion "to the magnitude of ordinary experience," and so widen our understanding of it. Bergen Evans underscores the danger present in all analogies when he says that "the inferring of a further degree of resemblance from an observed degree is one of the greatest pitfalls of popular thinking."[1] The fallacy comes in when we use an analogy in lieu of proof, read more into it than the facts warrant, and note only similarities while ignoring differences.

Often we unintentionally deceive ourselves in this way. But analyzing similarities and differences correctly is a prime tool of learning. Without it we could not build on experience and relate new knowledge to old. We study a strange proposition or picture or problem, and ask: "What in this new situation is like something I have seen before? What is unfamiliar?" To learn, we have to concentrate on the new and different aspects. But the analogy-monger tends to ignore the differences, and push the similarities to an unjustified extreme.

[1] *Natural History of Nonsense.*

Broadly interpreted, the field of analogy includes metaphors, folk sayings, and the practice of sympathetic magic, whether employed by primitive peoples or by modern consumers of the more exotic brands of patent medicines. It extends into education; indeed it would be impossible to bring up children without a frequent use of analogies to relate their limited first-hand experience to wider knowledge. "Yes, dear, a skunk is like a kitty but—" "No, Roger, the wings of a plane are not like the wings of a bird except for soaring—"

All human talk, even the most learned philosophical discussion, is packed with metaphors. Open a page of any book to find: "*root* of the problem," "*falling* into error," "*steps* to take," "*packed* with metaphors." But metaphors are not explicitly formulated analogies, for we use them unconsciously. Many have become cemented (there we go) into the language over the centuries, and these are seldom used to clinch (another one) our argument.

Folk sayings, many of which we shall meet in Chapter 15 as "self-evident truths," often are cast in the form of analogies. A favorite tag today is, "Where there's smoke there's fire." If a person has been accused, for example, of disloyalty on a mere rumor, the absence of proof does not clear him. Neighbors shake their heads, employers turn him down. "Where there's smoke," they say, "there must be fire."

The "sympathetic magic" of primitive peoples is based on reasoning by analogy. You make a doll in the image of your enemy, transfix it with a bone arrow, and lo, following the proper incantations by the medicine man, your enemy becomes very sick indeed, at least in theory. The "doctrine of signatures" in early medicine followed a similar pattern. Powdered walnuts were administered for diseases of the brain

because walnuts were convoluted like the brain. *Eyebright,*
a plant marked with a spot resembling the human eye, was of
course the specific for afflictions of the eye, while *celandine,*
a plant with yellow juice, was confidently prescribed for
jaundice.

FORMOSA EQUALS MUNICH

Our chief concern in this chapter is not with figures of
speech or ceremonial rites but with consciously formulated
analogies supposed to clarify current happenings. Under closer
examination they may be found to do nothing of the kind·
they darken rather than illumine, like the radar "wall."

In the spring of 1955, Americans were trying to understand
what was going on in the Formosa Straits. Tension and fear
were in the air. Would the Red Chinese attack the offshore
islands? Would we retaliate if they did? Would the action
kindle a new world war? Editorial writers, radio commentators,
columnists, letter writers to the papers, philosophers in bars
and grills, began aiming analogies in all directions. The favorite
took the form: "If the U.S. backs down it will be Munich all
over again!" Prime Minister Neville Chamberlain, it was remembered, had let Czecho-Slovakia go to Hitler at Munich
without a fight. The symbol of the surrender had become his
umbrella. Senator Knowland of California used the Munich
analogy with vigor:[2]

> There are still some who believe that the way to deal with an
> international bully is by appeasement. At Munich the world should
> have learned that the road to appeasement is not the road to peace.
> It is surrender on the installment plan.

An angry letter writer cried that Red China had consistently
broken the Korean truce, so what keeps us from attacking her?
The peace in our time, which Chamberlain thought he brought

[2] New York *Herald Tribune,* May 13, 1955.

home from Munich, was too high a price to pay for trying to stop World War II. If we agree to a cease-fire in the Formosa Straits, the letter writer continued, it is too high a price to pay for the "loss of all Asia and the isolation of our country in a yellow tide."

These bristling analogies about Munich—with a thin entering wedge on the end—follow the stereotype that "history teaches." Nothing in the flow of human affairs, of course, repeats itself precisely, and a truer saying is that "history is an irreversible process." The circumstances of Munich, in the middle of Europe in 1938, were vastly different from those off the China coast in 1955. For one thing, the atomic bomb had not been invented. Yet when President Eisenhower and his staff landed at the Washington airport in a rainstorm after the Geneva Conference of July 1955, they found themselves thoroughly drenched. Considerably to their astonishment no one offered them an umbrella; all umbrellas had been banned as too reminiscent of Munich!

"You say the Chinese Reds are Communists? Why, they are nothing but Agrarian Reformers." This analogy was widely accepted just before the peace-loving agrarians drove our ally Chiang Kai-shek clean off the Asiatic continent.

A lady letter writer draws a parallel between the Reds and a local marauder. The Reds, she says, stole China from Chiang implying that China was the Generalissimo's personal possession. "Would you relinquish a claim to your property because a thief stole it from you?" she asks heatedly, apparently confusing the property laws of Montclair, New Jersey, with international power politics. If we had a world government and a world policeman the lady might have a point—but one suspects that these might alarm her even more.

Political democracy is sometimes compared to a ship, where citizens as sailors pull on the ropes with a yo ho ho together. This is a miserable parallel, for the captain of a ship is still an absolute dictator in emergencies, with powers of life and death.

Another popular analogy concerns the thirteen American colonies in 1787. If they were able to compose their many differences, it is argued, and adopt a Constitution, why can't the quarreling nations of the world get together and adopt a World Constitution? At first hearing, the argument is persuasive. Then we remember that the American colonies had one language, one culture, on Christian religion, and one compact location. The eighty quarreling nations have no such solid foundation on which to build.

In Marquand's novel, *So Little Time*, guests at a cocktail party in 1941 are discussing the fall of France. "Just now everyone was saying that we were like France, that if we didn't wake up, we would end just like France. It makes no sense, because America was not like France. . . ." Among other major differences was a three-thousand-mile stretch of salt water, separating America from Germany.

Before World War II, many writers, including your author, often discussed the economic and social problems of America by drawing parallels with France, Britain, Germany, Sweden. Ah, Sweden, what a landmark for reformers! Now we know that those comparisons were way out of line. The U.S. in 1940 was a different organism—bigger, more self-sufficient, more productive, less experienced, racially more mixed—than the small countries of western Europe.

A writer for the *Freeman* in 1955 produced a regular blockbuster of an analogy—my favorite horrible example to date—in the debate on U.S. foreign policy. He equated a policy of coexistence with Russia, with Chamberlain's policy at Munich, with Roosevelt's at Yalta, Truman's at Potsdam, Eisenhower's cease-fire in Korea, with Mendès-France at Geneva giving up North Vietnam. Here, says this savant, "is the true measure of the morality of the coexistence policy!"

AN INSTITUTION IS NOT A PERSON

Drawing parallels between an institution and an individual is a risky business. Like the lady letter writer who equated the loss of China with a second-story man in Montclair, is the soapbox orator in London's famous Hyde Park. The speaker put the following question to his audience: "How does Winston Churchill propose to build three hundred thousand houses a year in his postwar housing program, when it took him five years to build one brick wall at his country place?"

Churchill built the wall with his own hands as a hobby, but his housing program was to be designed and financed by the British Government, and built by hundreds of thousands of craftsmen and laborers. There is no legitimate comparison, but the soapboxer probably scored a point.

Politicians of both parties have long assured us that the U.S. national debt is exactly like a mortgage on our home. Both are heavy burdens, they say, and should be paid off at the earliest possible moment. We are not told that the national debt is a source of investment and income for banks, insurance companies, trust funds, foundations, and individual holders of government bonds. We are not told that any attempt to liquidate it suddenly would wreck the U.S. financial system. We are not told that experts who manage the national debt must use very different rules from householders trying to pay off the mortgage.

Meanwhile lawyers and courts have had endless trouble with the legal fiction that a corporation is a person; that the Standard Oil Company of New Jersey is just like you and me.

A letter writer argues that "Parity is the farmer's minimum wage law. What could possibly be 'high' about wages or prices which are only 90 percent of the minimum?" The editor of the *New York Times* pounces on the analogy. The purpose of the minimum wage law, he says, is to protect workers at, or near, the subsistence level; it is flexible, and affects only a small number of the total labor force. High, rigid price supports for farmers haven't the faintest resemblance to minimum wages. "It is because it is the antithesis of the latter that we are opposed to it." Parity may have respectable arguments in its favor, but the *Times* very properly throws out this one.

Attic inventors, when shunned by investors, have a well-rehearsed response: "Look at Fulton," they say, "look at Edison, look at Alexander Graham Bell. Everybody laughed at the first steamboat, the first phonograph, the first telephone. This little supercharger of mine is going to be even more important!" People did laugh at Fulton and Edison, true enough, and I wish my grandfather had not laughed at Alexander Graham Bell when he could have got in on the ground floor. But for every invention which survived public merriment, it is safe to say that a thousand were laughed permanently and properly out of court.

A letter writer to the *New York Times* remembers arguing with a woman pacifist at a dinner party. "When I asked her if she would fight if I tried to throw her baby out of the window, she turned angrily away. . . ." The lady should have done more than turn away, she should have poured the soup over his head, and the hotter the better! This is one of those gross, below-the-belt arguments, on a par with "Do you want your daughter to marry a Negro?" The issue is jerked out of context and put on a savage personal level, utterly beyond intelligent discussion.

Analogies are cardinal to human thinking. They add depth and perspective to current experience. But they should be handled responsibly, or clarification may turn into confusion and worse. Open your newspaper to "Letters to the Editor" and it will be an off day when you do not find an example that is misleading, unjust, thoroughly fallacious, or all three.

11

Wise Men Can Be Wrong

Fallacy Number Seven

**AD
VERECUNDIAM**

A FAMOUS *New Yorker* cartoon shows a well-upholstered lady at breakfast in her Park Avenue apartment, opening the morning paper. "I never know what to think," she is saying, "until I've read Walter Lippmann." Mr. Lippmann can help to steady anyone's thoughts about China or France or Senate investigations, but he should not be made responsible for the whole job.

So great was the reverence for the name of Aristotle that a medieval scholar could win almost any argument by citing a text which indicated that *the* philosopher agreed with him.[1] The loser in these tournaments must have been considerably annoyed, and one might hazard the guess that the fallacy known as *ad verecundiam* was discovered then and there. As late as 1600, students at the Sorbonne were commanded to follow the texts of Aristotle or suffer dreadful penalties.

Ad verecundiam means "appeal to revered authority." It is listed among the classic fallacies and its simplicity is deceptive. Quoting authorities is of course entirely legitimate, and only when pushed too far, when the Big Name freezes mental activity, does it become a fallacy. It is not so much that one

[1] Abelard referred to him as "our saint Aristotle."

89

thinks wrongly, as that one ceases to think at all. The appeal is often to great figures (or documents) of the past, which have become symbols, stirring emotion rather than reason.

Authorities are of various kinds: Great Men, Great Books, great anonymous sayings immortalized in folklore, the practice known as "footnoting," and lately, "science says" and "statistics prove." In this chapter I will assemble cases dealing with Great Men, and with "footnoting." In the next chapter I will illustrate bogus appeals to the authority of "science" and "statistics."

"It says so in the Bible" is an old but continuing example of *ad verecundiam*. So is an appeal to the dictionary. David Guralnik, who engineered a drastic revision of *Webster*, once shocked an audience and shattered its faith in the dictionary's infallibility. Unlike certain brands of cigarettes, he said, supposed to be untouched by human hands, dictionaries are made by men, and the best of them contain mistakes.

Most American investors looked up to those bankers and financial wizards who convinced us, just before the crash of 1929, that the stock market had entered a new and permanent level of values. We trusted these wise men, and did not stop to analyze the ever more fantastic ratio of earnings to market prices.

Appeal to authority is very ancient, personified in the medicine man of the tribe. Its power over an individual begins early: "my daddy said so." A little later comes "my teacher said so," and "the minister said so." A sign used to be posted in British schools: "The teacher could be wrong. Think for yourselves." It illustrates as good a defense against *ad verecundiam* as anything I know.

We need to be on guard also against an authority which may be correct as far as it goes, but does not apply to the issue. It is not very helpful, for instance, to try to apply what

Caesar said about the use of foot soldiers to a military problem involving atomic weapons. Morris Cohen discriminates carefully between the two kinds of appeal to authority:

First: An appeal which is inevitable and reasonable. If we lack the time or energy to go into a matter thoroughly, we let an expert resolve it for us. But his authority should be only relative, not final; we should always reserve the right to check what he hands down.

Second: An appeal which invests some source with infallibility, very common in matters involving religion and moral conduct, and frequent in political and economic matters as well.

For some people Adam Smith or Karl Marx is as infallible as Aristotle used to be. Hitler looked to the stars for his authority and wrote *Mein Kampf.* Millions of Germans, frustrated by their troubles following World War I, looked to der Fuehrer as an infallible guide, and read *Mein Kampf* almost as a sacred text. The infallible guide led them into one of the greatest disasters which ever befell a nation.

TROUBLE FOR COLUMBUS

Columbus apparently went to his grave believing that the islands he had discovered in the Caribbean were the East Indies and that Cuba was an Asian peninsula. The belief is still recorded in the name West *Indies.* He had various reasons for his belief, all wrong, and one of the strongest was reliance on a scriptural authority.[2] In the second part of the Apocryphal Book of Ezra, the second verse of the sixth chapter reads: "Six parts hast Thou made dry." This was taken to mean that the world was six parts dry land to one part water.[3] Asia was known to be a huge continent, and there could not be a great

---

[2] From J. G. Leithauser, *Worlds Beyond the Horizon,* 1955.
[3] The true ratio is substantially the reverse of this

deal of water between Europe and Asia. Even the voyage from Spain to the Caribbean, Columbus felt, was longer than the Book of Ezra allowed. When he sighted land, accordingly, he was sure it must be Asia. Ezra, as a supplement to the Bible, is not much referred to today, but it was gospel to thinkers in the fifteenth century.

C. S. Forester, in his historical novel *To the Indies*, gives us another case of *ad verecundiam* based on Columbus. In his third voyage a Spanish lawyer named Don Narciso Rich has been assigned by the Crown to keep an eye on the Admiral's discoveries. Forester brings out the dramatic conflict in Columbus' mind, between the authority of the ancients and the new ways of science.

The little fleet comes to the island of Trinidad, and sails around it. Land is seen to the south. Columbus, consulting the works of Pliny, concludes that it must be another island, and sends Rich out in the longboat to investigate. Rich finds that the water five miles from shore is so fresh that the sailors can drink it. Fresh water, he reasons, means a river, and fresh water five miles out to sea means a great big river. Therefore, Rich concludes, the land to the south of Trinidad is probably a continent. His reasoning is sound, of course. Indians on shore tell him the river's name is Orinoco.

Rich comes back to report to Columbus. The admiral struggles with the account, as he tries to reconcile Pliny's four rivers—the Euphrates, Hiddekel, Pishon, and Gihon—with the Indian name Orinoco. Finally Columbus gives it up; reconciliation is impossible. Pliny cannot be wrong, and so the Orinoco does not exist.

FOUNDING FATHERS

The Founding Fathers are to American argument, especially political argument, what Pliny was to Columbus. A Columbia historian comments:

Since Revolutionary times, Americans have been appealing to their great men of old for support in political controversy. Now in a time of hesitation and anxiety they are carrying the practice to ridiculous extremes. Conservatives and liberals, reactionaries and radicals, absolutists and anarchists, conformists and heretics—all are heard to argue, not that the idea is wise, but that it would engage the support of great Americans of the past if they were alive today.[4]

Professor Rossiter finds at least seven Thomas Jeffersons now being appealed to as final authority for as many points of view. He gives specific quotations from Jefferson's writings to support each.

1. People opposed to Big Government and Statism cite him with reverence.

2. So do the people in favor of States' Rights.

3. So do Isolationists.

4. Agrarians, small farmers, lovers of the soil, quote with enthusiasm his criticisms of the sinful city.

5. Followers of science, reason, progress, find strong support in his writings.

6. People devoted to civil liberties and the Bill of Rights appeal to him constantly.

7. Believers in the democratic form of government—the People, Yes!—use Jefferson as their staunchest champion.

Some of these claims are in serious conflict. The extreme Right quotes him no less approvingly than the extreme Left. Did Jefferson therefore contradict himself? The truth seems to be that he had an active, inquiring mind and changed his point of view from time to time as new facts came in. As he was a prodigious letter writer and rarely failed to put in writing how he felt at the moment, he supplied devotees of *ad verecundiam* with stocks of quotations as ample as they were varied.

[4] Clinton Rossiter in the *Reporter*, December 15, 1955.

George Washington's warning against "foreign entangle-
ments" in his Farewell Address remains a prime favorite, despite
such new conditions as the hydrogen bomb, and the fact that
London is now nearer to New York, in travel hours, than Phila-
delphia was to New York in Washington's day.

An excited liberal writes to the New York *Herald Tribune*
protesting against the "power trust" and its alleged attempts
to fasten the label "creeping socialism" on all public power
projects. The same label should also be applied, he says, "to
such great Americans as George Washington, John Adams
and Thomas Jefferson, who believed that the great natural
resources of the nation should not be allowed to fall into the
hands of the few." This gives us another Jefferson, number
eight, conservationist and sponsor for public power!

A New York judge recently sentenced four sets of parents
to various terms in jail, while reading them a lecture on
juvenile delinquency. "It is time," he said, "that parents return
to the moral principles on which this Republic was founded."
He did not mention that when the Republic was founded,
New York City had a population of forty-nine thousand and
everything above Forty-second Street was farm land. The New
York of today, with its eight million people living in paved
canyons, exerts very different and far more ominous pressures
on young people.

"FOOTNOTING"

"Footnoting" means piling up references and documents
until the opposition is silenced by sheer tonnage. Senator
McCarthy was famous for staggering into the Senate Chamber
loaded like an Everest climber with files, reports, and papers,
which he pounded as he delivered one of his notable philippics.
Trial lawyers sometimes use a similar technique to impress
juries.

Richard Rovere once examined a bulky file of McCarthy's documents in the Senator's office, at the latter's request. In this file, which dealt with the Malmédy massacre in the Battle of the Bulge, Rovere could find no dependable evidence at all. But he admits, in his book *The Eisenhower Years*:

> I continued to be impressed by the Senator's manner. And the papers themselves were impressive—not only by virtue of their contents but by virtue of their existence. Photostats and carbon copies and well-kept newspaper clippings have, I think, an authority of their own for most people; we assume that no one would go to the bother of assembling them if they didn't prove something.

A true quotation can be torn out of context so that only part of the original is cited. Thus an advertisement for a new play may read, " 'Wonderful!'—*Evening Standard*"—when the *Standard's* reviewer actually said "a wonderful slice of pure ham."

Before me is a photograph of the chairman of the Atomic Energy Commission, surrounded by four large crates of documents, which have just been wheeled into the room where the Joint Congressional Atomic Energy Committee is holding a hearing on the Dixon-Yates contract for TVA power.[5] "Who is responsible for this physical display?" asks Senator Anderson of New Mexico with some asperity.

"I am," says the chairman, and explains that the crates contain papers on every subject *other* than Dixon-Yates. This proves, he says, that the Atomic Energy Commission has not slighted its study of weapons because of the power contract controversy. The file on Dixon-Yates is brought in next—a stack of papers about six inches high.

"I don't think we need this kind of physical display," exclaims Senator Pastore of Rhode Island. "I think this is assum-

[5] New York *Herald Tribune*, February 11, 1955.

ing an air of ridiculousness." Ridiculous or not, it assumes a decided air of *ad verecundiam,* department of footnoting.

When the Chinese Reds announced in 1954 that they were holding thirteen American fliers on espionage charges, they claimed that spying had been proved by "ten thousand pieces of evidence taken from the fliers." This works out to 769 pieces of evidence per man, presumably including suspender buttons.

A book loaded with footnotes seems to show that the author has consulted everybody since Confucius. What the author has to say, accordingly, must be so. Sometimes, however—as I have learned by experience in many libraries—he has only laid down a barrage of references to cover the thinness of his thoughts. F.C.S. Schiller remarks ironically that "nothing has a greater hold on the human mind than nonsense fortified with technicalities."

Cartoonist Webster's immortal character, Caspar Milquetoast, believes everything he sees in print, including signboards, sky writing, and magazine advertising. The dear man spends his life trying to follow instructions—instructions which frequently contradict each other and get him into endless trouble. He is the perfect victim of *ad verecundiam,* crediting every footnote, never checking sources, never allowing for differences in time, never daring to figure things out for himself.

12

"Figures Prove"

Fallacy Number Eight

IN *Life on the Mississippi* Mark Twain shows us what figures can do—if you combine them with imagination.

In the space of 176 years the Lower Mississippi has shortened itself 242 miles. This is an average of a trifle over one mile and a third per year. Therefore, any calm person, who is not blind or idiotic, can see that in the Old Silurian Period, just a million years ago next November, the River was upward of 1,300,000 miles long, and stuck out over the Gulf of Mexico like a fishing rod. And by the same token, any person can see that 742 years from now the Lower Mississippi will be only a mile and three-quarters long, and Cairo and New Orleans will have joined their streets together . . .

THE NEW AUTHORITY

A witty Frenchman once remarked that Americans like ice cream and statistics, as both slip down so easily. The more decimal places in the statistics, I might add, the easier they slip. What Aristotle symbolized to the ancients, and Pliny to Columbus, "science" and "statistics" represent to the modern generation. Science of course well merits our interest, for ever since Galileo it has been transforming the world. Without science, especially medical science, probably half the world's present population would not be alive. When legitimate interest in science turns to blind worship, however, we have another example of the logical fallacy of *ad vere-*

cundiam. Instead of bowing to the great man, we bow down
to four decimal places.

Favorite symbols for "science" are the microscope, the white
coat, the beard. When an advertiser decides to use this pitch
he gives us a picture of a stern-looking gentleman in a white
coat and Vandyke beard, peering down a microscope, with the
caption "Science Says . . ." The *New Yorker* reports that a
laboratory technician rushed into a barbershop on Fifty-eighth
Street to borrow a couple of coats. "Some advertising men are
up in the lab taking pictures," he explained. "They said we
had to get some white jackets to wear because scientists always
wear white jackets."

As an economist and accountant I have long been interested
in fallacious deductions from statistics. Another author, Darrell
Huff, has been interested enough to write a book about them.[1]
It is well worth reading in toto, as you will see from the samples
I shall presently quote. These fallacious deductions can be
classified in a number of ways, as noted in Chapter 9, where
statistical *post hocs* were examined with some care.[2] In the
present chapter we will ride a few dizzy curves into the
future—a form of travel known as extrapolation. We will
then look at various illegitimate deductions from figures and
scientific "laws."

RIDING CURVES

The Mark Twain story is a perfect case of dizzy extrapolation,
where a curve is ridden one million years into the past, and
742 years into the future. Riding it, Mark "proved" that the
Mississippi River did not belong on any real map—only in
Cloud-Cuckoo Land.

Take a piece of cross-section paper, and a copy of the
World Almanac, and with these plot the population of the

---

[1] *How to Lie with Statistics,* Norton, 1954.
[2] Cohen and Nagel list eleven kinds of statistical fallacies.

U.S. from 1800 to 1860. Look, it doubles every twenty years, no doubt about it. Let us climb aboard this curve. By 1940 it has reached 503 million people; by 1960 just over a billion! But the actual U.S. population in 1940, according to the Census, was only 131 million. More than seventy years ago, in his second message to Congress, Lincoln fell into a similar error. He predicted that by 1930, the U.S. population would reach 251,689,914. All the Census could actually find in 1930 was 122,775,046.

The Population Reference Bureau calculates that the percentage of Americans sixty-five years of age and over has doubled since 1900.[3] Along with this trend has gone an increase in the proportion of older women. All correct so far. Then the Bureau takes off into the wild blue yonder. "In terms of voting power, ownership of land, and common stocks, the U.S. can be seen on the road toward a gerontomatriarchy— control by aging females." Anthropologists have not yet found a society completely controlled by females, aging or otherwise, though they have located societies where the ceremonial killing of the aged is practiced.[4]

Huff cites a report that in the five years between 1947 and 1952, television sets in American homes increased about 10,000 percent. "Project this," he says, "for the next five years and you'll find there'll soon be a couple billion of the things, heaven forbid, or 40 sets per family." If you want to be even sillier, he says, take a base year earlier than 1947 and "prove" that every American family will soon have 40,000 TV sets.

A statistical fallacy closely allied with extrapolation concludes that if a certain cause produces a certain effect, then twice the cause will produce twice the effect. If a glass of milk is good for you, two glasses are twice as good. Maybe, but

[3] UP dispatch, May 8, 1955.
[4] Those Amazons, alas, were a discovery worthy of old Dr. Cook. Says Ralph Linton in *The Study of Man:* "It is questionable whether there is any society in existence which is completely dominated by women."

not five glasses. If one old-fashioned cocktail makes you feel fine, then ten will improve your well-being tenfold. More probably, however, they will make most people feel perfectly awful, assuming they can feel at all.

THE PROFIT ANGLE

Soon after I received my C.P.A. degree, I was retained to study the accounts of a large corporation. The company was claiming in a blaze of publicity that its profits were so small it was practically giving away the product. Net income was said to be a beggarly one cent for every dollar of sales. This did look modest indeed.

I found the figure correct—but not the conclusion. Digging deeper, I noted that average net earnings in recent years, measured against the company's investment, or net worth, were spectacular. Stockholders were earning far more than in other concerns in the same field. Thus the ratio of profit to sales was a true figure but irrelevant. In a business enterprise what really counts is the ratio of profit to *investment*.

By shifting the scale in drawing a chart you can favor an argument, while your opponent, by selecting another scale, can ruin it. Suppose you want to show profits rising like the Rocky Mountains. You make the dollar scale and the time scale like this:

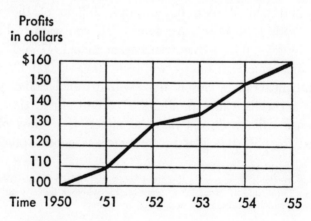

But your opponent wants to play down the profits. So he plots *exactly the same figures,* but with a wider time scale and a narrower dollar scale, like this:

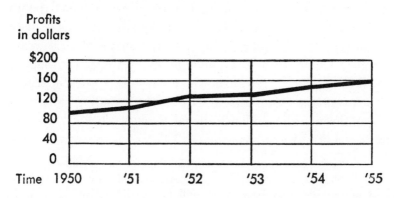

What a pedestrian showing for the period these "figures prove"!

Another joker lies in confusing an increase in *percentage* with an increase in *percentage points.* If your profits on investment go up from 5 percent one year to 10 percent the next, you have made a legitimate increase of 100 percent—an excellent showing on any set of books! But the same thing can be described with equal accuracy as "a rise of five percentage points"—which sounds like practically nothing at all.

Polls of public opinion have been known to confuse percentages with percentage points. They have also been known to drop the "D.K.'s," "don't knows," down the trap door in reporting results. For example, suppose 40 percent of respondents say "yes," 10 percent say "no," and 50 percent say "don't know." If a pollster throws out the "don't knows" and reports that 80 percent of the people are in favor and only 20 percent opposed, he gravely distorts the actual situation.[5]

A favorite statistical pastime in late December is forecasting business conditions for the new year. The experts toss in their

[5] Responsible pollsters guard against these errors.

predictions, while businessmen listen spellbound. If the consensus of expert opinion is for a 10 percent rise, a smart operator may predict an increase of 11.53 percent. Not only does this figure top the field, but those two decimal points look most authoritative. He could equally well have used seventeen decimal places, and still the shape of next year's business would be only a guess. So many things can happen tomorrow which are unknown today—wars, peace scares, new inventions, storms, floods, strikes, the unending foolishness of politicians. The Valley National Bank of Phoenix, Arizona, in an ironical prospectus issued in 1954 put it this way:

The most dependable forecast that anyone can make regarding 1955 is that, irrespective of what happens between now and the end of the year, all forecasters will be predicting an increase in business in 1956.

As I write this chapter, late in December, 1955, all the forecasters, except a few terrible-tempered Mr. Bangses, are predicting a roaring business for 1956.

DECIMAL PLACES

Decimal places exert an uncanny fascination, and the more there are the more impressive they appear. A graduate student in psychology aspiring for a master's degree may send out this questionnaire:

In eating pickles would you say you
              ( )   Like them very much
              ( )   Like them somewhat
              ( )   Are indifferent to them
              ( )   Dislike them mildly
              ( )   Dislike them intensely

Please check the statement that comes nearest to your feeling about pickles.

He sends it to 5,000 addresses and gets 470 replies, divided, in the order shown above: 108, 82, 67, 95, 118. From these data it is legitimate to conclude that of the people who answered, slightly more dislike pickles than like them, and that's about all one can conclude. But our student boldly goes ahead. He sends his data to the calculating department of the university and receives the following results:

Strongly for pickles	22.98%
Mildly for pickles	17.45
Indifferent to pickles	14.25
Mildly against pickles	20.21
Strongly against pickles	25.11
Total	100.00%

It is easy to be impressed with these decimal places, all adding up neatly to 100.00 percent. But our student has never looked behind his figure to the actual human picture, where most of his list throw the questionnaire in the wastebasket with a snort, and where those who do answer tap their teeth with a pencil trying to make up their minds how in hell they do feel about pickles.

Figures are never any better than the physical data on which they are based, and stringing out the decimal places only serves to camouflage the error. In the pickles case, the physical data are subjective, uncertain, and incomplete. But it is no worse than some other figuring which consumes a good many man-years in our universities, and often applies to more important matters than pickles.

ASK FOR A BREAKDOWN

Huff cites an argument about fatal accidents due to motorcars compared to railroads. Everyone present agrees that the automobile tops the field, but Mr. A. claims that the railroads hardly ever kill anyone nowadays. Mr. B. counters with the report that they killed 4,712 persons last year, not including railroad employees. His figure is correct, and looks like a long way from "hardly anyone."

Mr. A., obviously a student of logical fallacies, demands a breakdown—what we should all request in such cases. The breakdown discloses that half the railroad victims were motorists who tried to argue with a locomotive at grade crossings, and most of the other half were riding the rods. Only 132 of the 4,712 fatalities were bona fide passengers. Thus Mr. A. has the best of the argument in the end—railroads kill relatively few ticket holders.

The high command of the Republican party seems to be following Mr. B. Recently it reported 8,008 government employees dismissed for "reasons of security." One major implication was that they were all Communists, with the further implication that the administration had been vigilant in rooting the subversives out. A breakdown, however, indicated that only a tiny fraction of the 8,008 had been fired for actual disloyalty. Political opponents call this kind of reporting the "numbers game," and logicians might call it a genuine *ad verecundiam*, where figures appear to prove something very different from the facts.

Huff tells how a national labor organization showed a chart with index numbers for corporation profits rising much more rapidly than index numbers for wages, after the depression of the thirties. The figures were correct, and at first glance it looked as if the downtrodden worker had been stepped on once again. A second glance, however, disclosed the fallacy of the reasoning. At the bottom of the depression, corporate profits as a class were in the red, but wages, while low, were still being paid. As better times crept back, the index of profits was bound to go up much more steeply than the index of wages.

Speaking of wages, the fast operator in statistics can always have a field day with *averages*. Let us take a very simple case, involving the income of everybody in a small business. The proprietor is accused of paying starvation wages. He replies that the average income for those working in his business is $3,000—not so bad. But a breakdown shows:

1 Proprietor	$20,000	
1 Office worker	2,000	
8 Shop workers	8,000	(or $1,000 each)
10 workers get	$30,000	

The average, to be sure, is $3,000, but no one except the boss receives as much as that.

An "average of averages" can scramble things up even more. One of the first rules I learned as a cub accountant was to shy violently at an average of averages. Here is a case:

In a class of 10 children, 3 boys and 7 girls take a test in arithmetic. The boys average 70 percent; the girls average 90 percent. What is the average for the class?

If we average the averages, we get 80 percent for the class. (70+90=160, divided by 2=80)

But if we see the pitfall, we calculate the class average at the *correct figure of 84 percent*. (3 boys at 70=210,+7 girls at 90=630. 210+630=840, divided by 10=84)

A recruiting sergeant citing figures can convince most people that the death rate in the U.S. Army in war is less than the death rate in any big American city during the same period. "So enlist, you so-and-so's, and keep healthy!" What the sergeant fails to mention is that the city death rate includes sick people, old people, and infants, while the army death rate is based on healthy young men between eighteen and thirty-five.

DANGER: MEN FIGURING

After reviewing a large number of statistical fallacies, Huff gives us five trenchant warnings. Before meekly accepting a deduction from any set of figures, ask yourself:

1. Who says so?
2. How does he know?
3. What's missing?
4. Did somebody change the subject—
   i.e., shift the base, or the scale?
5. Does it make sense?

To which I might add that no figures are better than the original data, whatever the number of decimal places.

After developing his magnificent concept of proof, Pythagoras fell into the dismal swamp of mystic numbers—especially number 7. Some economic statisticians seem to be following him with their mystic index numbers for "production in general," including everything a nation produces, from apples to locomotives.[6] The more complicated the mathematical systems of averaging, chaining, and least squares, the more dubious the result. Mathematics cannot legitimately be used to jam together on paper things which are never jammed in the outside world except in freight-train wrecks.

The authority of mathematics was once used with devastating success at the Russian Court in the days of Catherine the Great.[7] The Empress was alarmed by the visit of Diderot, encyclopedist and materialist, and feared that he might undermine the faith of her court retainers. So she asked the noted mathematician Euler to put Diderot in his place. The Court was summoned to hear the debate. Euler led off by informing

---

[6] See *Horses and Apples*, by Bassett Jones (John Day, 1934).
[7] Lancelot Hogben, *Mathematics for the Million* (Norton, 1937).

his opponent that the existence of God had been conclusively established. The proof lay, he said, in the equation:

$$\frac{a+b^n}{n} = x$$

"Donc Dieu existe—répondez!"—Therefore God exists—reply!

Diderot was as terrified as any American college freshman by this equation. Instead of replying he fled the assembly, shut himself up in his chambers, and demanded a safe-conduct back to France.

And here is a practical mathematician from Britain. A roadside merchant was asked how he could sell rabbit sandwiches so cheaply. He replied: "Well, I have put in some horse meat too. But I mix 'em strictly fifty-fifty: one horse, one rabbit."

13

Appeal to the Crowd

Fallacy Number Nine

> **AD POPULUM**

AT THE Democratic National Convention of 1896, strong men are said to have fainted when William Jennings Bryan, candidate for President, reached his peroration:

> You shall not press down upon the brow of labor this crown of thorn. You shall not crucify mankind upon a cross of gold!

The speech was compared favorably with the best efforts of Demosthenes, Cicero, and Daniel Webster, and won Bryan the nomination, though not the election. Now we know that it was pure political hokum, bolstering a very dubious economic argument for the free coinage of silver with an appeal to (1) the symbol of the noble working man, and (2) the symbol of the crucifixion.

Some years earlier a deputation of Protestant clergymen in New York waited upon James G. Blaine, the Republican candidate for President. Their spokesman, one Samuel Dicker-man Burchard, cut himself another generous slice of hokum, now found in the history books:

> We are Republicans, and don't propose to leave our party and identify ourselves with the party whose antecedents have been Rum, Romanism and Rebellion.

The Reverend Mr. Burchard was of course referring to the Democrats, who were not ardent advocates of Prohibition, who were supported by much of the Catholic vote in large cities, and had advocated slavery below the Mason and Dixon line before the Civil War. His three R's spread like wildfire in the campaign.

President Theodore Roosevelt, a Republican, lashed out at "malefactors of great wealth" in a speech at Provincetown in 1907. In 1933 Franklin D. Roosevelt, Democrat, advocated "driving the money-changers out of the temple," and, like Bryan, stepped up his appeal by a theological reference.

ARGUMENTUM AD POPULUM

This fallacy is an attempt to win an argument by an appeal to the crowd, the mass, the mob, rather than by reason. If it has somewhat snobbish overtones, we should remember that it was defined by the classicists long before the rise of democracy in our modern sense. Even in this country, as late as the early 1800's, Alexander Hamilton exclaimed: "Your people, sir, is a great beast."

Every society has its popular credos, myths, and systems of belief, varying slowly with time, and also with the subgroups inside the society. The beliefs of farmers differ somewhat from those of city-dwellers, as the Romans well knew. The fallacy of *ad populum* arises when a political or social issue is argued not on its merits, but by an emotional appeal to a popular view or a slogan.

Ad populum could be classified as a branch of propaganda, and the fallacy is indeed widely used in propaganda. But the latter, as we shall develop it in Chapters 20 and 21, is not only more comprehensive but more cynical. Bryan, for all his incandescent verbiage, really believed in the doctrine of free silver, while the hard-boiled propagandist rarely believes in anything but himself. *Ad populum,* too, as one of the classic fallacies, was identified long before the advent of the mass media—without which modern propaganda could not get off the ground.

There are two large groups in America susceptible to *ad populum* appeals: (1) the rank and file of citizens, with modest incomes, and (2) the "Main Street" group, with somewhat higher incomes. Persons with incomes above twelve thousand dollars a year are relatively too small a class to warrant a "popular" appeal. Bryan sought to influence the rank and file and so did the two Roosevelts, in the above quotations. The Reverend Mr. Burchard was aiming more at Main Street with his striking alliteration of "Rum, Romanism and Rebellion."

RANK-AND-FILE SYMBOLS

"The voice of the people," said Bryan again, quoting a Latin tag, "is the Voice of God." The Great Commoner seldom failed to grasp any celestial hand available. His rival, President McKinley, was more mundane, but perhaps equally effective, when he proffered "The Full Dinner Pail" to the workers.

As the rank and file tended to resent the more affluent, the symbolism addressed to them ran to attacks on "The Trusts," "Monopolists," "Profiteers," "Vested Interests," "Plutocrats," "Wall Street," and "Bloated Bond Holders." Here, for instance, is a cartoon drawn by Art Young for the 1912 presidential campaign, which shows "capitalism" as a vast, bloated hog, crushing the whole countryside, with the caption "Time to Butcher."

Today in 1956, with full employment, a car, electric gadgets, and TV in most American homes, the symbolism is showing serious signs of wear and tear. A nation-wide survey in 1954 by the Institute of Social Relations at Michigan University, indicated that some three quarters of all Americans, while hardly enamored of "Big Business," felt that large American corporations, on balance, had done more good than harm. Art Young's cartoon would be meaningless to the rank and file of 1956.

MAIN STREET'S SYMBOLS

The Main Street group is smaller in numbers, but its spokesmen today are more vocal. They speak primarily for the business community, and their symbols, both positive and negative, are many and colorful. The "Middletown" study listed more than a hundred Main Street credos in the 1930's, most of them still in vigorous use.[1] The "Pauper Labor of Europe" is perhaps fading, together with "Bombs and Free Love." "Widows and Orphans," a once popular warning against taxes on inheritances and corporate profits (widows and orphans would suffer, if not starve) is no longer heard.

The conservative debater, however, can still denounce "Labor Agitators Who Should Go Back Where They Came From," "Government Interference," "Welfare State," "Socialized Medicine," "Bureaucracy and Red Tape," "Tinkering with the Currency," "Spending," "Handouts," and "Down the Rat-Hole of Europe." Considerable mileage also remains in "You Can't Change Human Nature."

On the approved side, "The Gold Standard" has lost some of its appeal, but "Our Free Enterprise System" and "Balance the Budget," draw highly favorable responses. At the moment, the latter seems perhaps the loftiest phrase in the whole litany of Main Street.

As a C.P.A. who once did some work on the federal budget, I marvel at how it has ceased to be an accounting matter, to become instead largely a doctrinal if not a theological matter. Not one American in a thousand, I am sure, understands the

[1] Robert and Helen Lynd.

distinction between a cash budget, an accrued budget carrying receivables and payables, and a capital budget, where long-term earning assets are excluded from annual income and outgo. These technical considerations, so essential to a proper fiscal policy, are submerged in a single credo, charged with emotion: "Balance the Budget!" What budget? When? At whose cost? Such questions are almost never asked.

DON GIUSTINO GOES INTO ACTION

Norman Douglas, in his famous satire *South Wind*, gives us a caricature of the demagogic lawyer, larding his case with appeals to popular prejudice and emotion. An Englishman has been murdered on the island of Nepenthe—which might be Capri—off the Italian coast. Signor Malipizzo, the local magistrate, has apprehended a half-witted boy as the murderer, and he feels that he needs a conviction to consolidate his position. His enemies meanwhile retain the great politico-lawyer Don Giustino from the mainland to defend the accused.

The courtroom is packed. Don Giustino begins in a voice so low that the audience must lean forward to hear him. "What a lovely place is your fair island of Nepenthe," he says. What a fortunate escape you have had from destruction by the volcano across the bay. It was nothing less than divine intervention by your Patron Saint which saved you! Your fertile fields are intact, the crops unhurt. Fathers can return at eve to gather round the family board. Family life, the sacred hearth! This poor lad had a mother. Ah, motherhood!

By this time many in the audience are choking up—even though the poor lad happens to be an orphan, his mother unknown. Somebody whispers this fact to Don Giustino, and without a pause he reverses his direction. To rescue a mother-less young soul, he says, from the brink of perdition is the noblest task of a Christian. Thank God this is still a Christian country in spite of the plots of heretics and unbelievers! Down with all foreigners! We know what they are and how they work for evil high and low. . . . They contaminate our land with their Godless depravity . . . a pest, a contagion. . . .

Don Giustino's famous vocal cords roll out a climax against marplots, especially those of English origin. The great Deputy ceases to speak. Signor Malipizzo has swooned away and the case is won! The accused lad is free. (He was innocent all along.)

I have paraphrased only a little of this masterpiece, but enough to show that Don Giustino has appealed to no less than ten symbols shared by the people of Nepenthe: the Homeland, the Patron Saint, the Fertile Earth, the Family at eve around the Sacred Hearth, Motherhood, pity for Orphans, the Christian religion, down with Unbelievers, down with Foreigners. Eight are positive, two negative, and he did not fail to sound the conspiracy note—Unbelievers and Foreigners plotting to destroy us. It would be difficult to find a more comprehensive illustration of *ad populum*. The real issue of the boy's guilt or innocence is lost in a thick fog of symbolism.

"THEY"

"They say the Russians are ready to revolt." "They say that necklines will be lower." "They say that Truman wants to run again." "They say a flying saucer landed in California and little green men came out."

It does no good to ask who "they" are. "They" are as nameless as they are infallible. "I heard it on the radio." "It said so in the paper." "I saw an article somewhere. . . ." This is as much documentation as one is likely to get. It is an appeal to bogus authority, for the locus can never be fixed. "They" sit like gods on Olympus, seeing all, knowing all, beyond mortal ken. People who rely most strongly on "they" read few books and have never heard of checking sources. "They" always preserve anonymity, for to name a "they" is, by defini· tion, to destroy him. Even if the appeal is to a ghostly authority, can we call it *ad verecundiam*? No, for I think the phenomenon is closer to *ad populum*. "They" are a symbol too, and a powerful one.

The Navy calls it "scuttlebutt." The layman terms it "grapevine." The housewife says it's "gossip." But in every case it is accepted as sheer gospel. Why? Because "They" said it was so. And who is "They"? The Admiral? The President? The storekeeper? Sh-sh! Don't say. For that would spoil it all by making you think. Keep it general. Keep it indefinite. Blame it on "They."[2]

The fallacy of *ad populum*, like "they," is a device to bypass independent thinking. The sight or the sound of symbols triggers the mind to run in well-worn emotional grooves and reach well-worn conclusions.

[2] From *Purchasing*, a house organ, 205 E. 42nd St., New York City.

14

Arguing in Circles

Fallacy Number Ten

**CIRCULUS
IN PROBANDO**

SOME disciples of Mahomet are said to advance the proposition that their holy book, the Koran, is infallible.

"Why?" it is asked.

"Because it was written by Allah's Prophet."

"How do you know that Mahomet is Allah's Prophet?"

"Because it says so in the Koran."

Retreating from Mecca to Main Street, two men go into a bank. One steps up to the paying teller's window and asks if he can cash a check.

"Who can identify you?" asks the teller.

"My friend here," says the man.

"But I don't know your friend."

"That's O.K., I'll introduce you."[1]

These are two examples of the logical fallacy, *circulus in probando*, or arguing in a circle. What looks like proof, or a valid conclusion, turns out, on closer inspection, to be saying the same thing. The conclusion is neatly inserted into the premises, and the argument boils down to: "It must be true because it says so itself."

[1] Lionel Ruby, *The Art of Making Sense.*

115

In a valid syllogism the two premises, major and minor, are triangulation points from which a logical conclusion can be drawn, as in the standard:

All men are mortal—major.
Socrates is a man—minor.
Therefore Socrates is mortal—conclusion.

You go forward, you get somewhere; but in a *circulus* you go round and round. At the end of the argument you know no more than at the beginning. The process reminds us of Fitzgerald's famous lines:

> Myself when young did eagerly frequent
> Doctor and Saint, and heard great Argument
>   About it and about: but evermore
> Came out by the same Door as in I went.

If the argument assumes as a premise the thing it claims to prove, obviously it proves nothing at all.

Chase has written several books on economics because he is an authority.
Chase is an authority on economics because he has written several books.

Round and round, proving nothing about Chase. And the following proves nothing about the glamorous Miss Z.:

This actress is on Broadway because she is famous.
She is famous because she is on Broadway.

Nor does a radio plug prove anything about "Savarin, the Coffier Coffee. It gives you more flavor because it has more flavor to give."

Nietzsche once declared that all mankind was corrupt. To a request for proof he answered: "The mere fact that you disagree with me is in itself proof that you are corrupted."[2]

[2] From Ruby.

The great iconoclast thus made his proposition airtight by calling anyone corrupt who challenged it. A wonderful system if you can get away with it. Many do, and probably most of us try from time to time.

Theological arguments, such as the case of the Koran above, make particular use of the fallacy. A religious sect, for instance, claims that no true believer will ever die. When somebody points out a normal death rate among the faithful, members retort that those who died were not true believers.

"How do you know?"

"Because they died."

An old-time argument "proving" the inferiority of the colored races takes the form: "Man is made in the image of God; since it is well known that God is not colored, it follows that a colored person is not a man." A perfect *circulus*.

MORAL BEES

A traveler is visiting a fetish priest in the African Congo.[3] Somewhat to his surprise he finds a box of live bees in his room. He asks the reason and the priest says: "If you had been an enemy those bees would have buzzed you out of here. Only last week a man came here with evil intentions. Those bees drove him out, he ran away screaming."

"What did the man say to you?"

"Nothing. He didn't have a chance."

"Then how do you know he had evil intentions?"

"Because the bees attacked him!"

Under analysis we find two propositions here:

(1) These bees attack only persons with evil intentions; proof: they attacked A, B, C, D. . . .

(2) A, B, C, D are persons with evil intentions; proof: the bees attack only such persons.

[3] Richard Wright, *Black Power* (Harper, 1954).

The fetish priest assumes a moral sense in honeybees. Presumably a man with good intentions could hit the hive with a hammer without arousing it. This story not only illustrates the fallacy of arguing in circles, but shows that natives along the Congo think much like the natives along the Hudson and the Thames.

A fortuneteller said to a client:

"Your son will be famous if he lives long enough!"

"What will he be famous for?"

"For having lived so long!"

The story does not say whether the client paid the fee, but probably she did.

Jeremy Bentham once pointed out that the fallacy of arguing in circles may lurk in a single word, and gave as an example a measure which was condemned on the ground that it was "un-English." If Bentham were alive today he could collect some prime examples in the current charge of "un-American" as sole proof of seditious behavior.

CIRCULUS FOR STALIN

At the 1934 Congress of the All-Union Communist party, the late and unlamented Joseph Stalin reported a conversation with the manager of one of the collective farms.[4]

Stalin—"How are you getting on with the sowing?"

Manager—"With the sowing, Comrade Stalin? We have mobilized ourselves!"

"Well, and what then?"

"We have put the question bluntly."

"And what next?"

"There is a turn, Comrade Stalin; soon there will be a turn."

"But still?"

"We can observe some progress."

[4] J. H. Spigelman in *Harper's Magazine*, September, 1955.

"But for all that, how are you getting on with the sowing?"

"Nothing has come of the sowing as yet, Comrade Stalin."

The poor fellow is back where he started from. Let us hope that his next move was not to Siberia.

Turning from agriculture to music, here is a typical after-concert argument. Mr. A. starts off with the declaration that classical music is better than modern music.

Miss B.: "How do you know it is?"

Mr. A.: "All the best critics say so."

Miss B.: "Who are the best critics?"

Mr. A.: "Those who appreciate the classics."

The original statement, as in many circular arguments, cannot be proved at all by deduction, for it concerns the subjective feelings of the individual listener. Feelings often enter these circles, which can express wishful thinking to perfection. The child who says, "I need it because I need it," may think he has given a reason. The true believer in the Koran thinks so too.

FLYING SAUCERS

The *Saturday Review* in 1955 ran an omnibus review of books about flying saucers. Some pretend to be scientific; others are apparently aimed at people with pretty low IQ's. The reviewer presently identified a pendulum type of reasoning. Said he: "One way for a reader to test the degree of nonsense contained in a typical book is to examine the bibliography carefully. There he will find a mutual admiration society among flying-saucer writers who cross-reference one another for substantiation." If we ask Author X: "What proof have you that the little men landed in Fresno, California?" he replies: "Author Y confirms it!" And when we ask Author Y for his proof, he declares: "X confirms it!"

In this mutual defense society, two propositions, neither of which has been proved true, are used alternately to "prove" each other. The way to break up such a *circulus*, observes Schiller, is to "extract the two propositions and display their interdependence."

Fast-working promoters have been known to employ a technique not too remote from this. The promoter, let us say, wants capital for his wingless airplane and a Big Name to launch it. So he goes to the man with the money and says the Big Name has come in, and he goes to the Big Name and says the money has come in. With luck they both succumb.

IRISH BULLS

Arguing in circles always involves a truism, or tautology. Although there is no proof, at the same time there is no disproof; a rose may indeed be a rose. Irish bulls, which are often discussed with the circular fallacy, deny the truism and contradict themselves; a rose is *not* a rose.

"All men are equal, but some are more equal than others"—which boils down to "equal men are unequal."

At a Washington hearing a Senator once exclaimed: "This is the most unheard-of thing I ever heard of."

"One of Peg Slattery's few witty remarks of record was her widely quoted comment that the only thing she liked about the Roosevelts was that they were Democrats, and she hated Democrats."[5] Putting this through the syllogistic sausage machine:

Peg hates Democrats.
The Roosevelts are Democrats.
Therefore Peg hates the Roosevelts.
P.S. But she likes the Roosevelts because they give her such a fine target to hate.

[5] John O'Hara in *Ten North Frederick* (Random House, 1955).

Pat Flaherty's friends ran him along to a banquet in a sedan chair which had no bottom. Said Pat, "Faith, and if it wuzznt fer the honor of the thing, oi moight jist as well've coom on fhoot."[6]

Irish bulls are usually visible a mile away, giving us plenty of time to climb a tree, chuckling as we climb. Circular arguments are not always so readily detected or so funny.

[6] From J. G. Brennan.

15

"Self-evident Truths"

Fallacy Number Eleven

LOGICAL arguments, as emphasized earlier, depend on certain assumptions or premises. If the premises are false, or are such that they cannot be verified, the conclusion does not carry much weight. The London *Economist* once neatly impaled this type of logic when it criticized a financial writer for "proceeding from an unwarranted assumption to a foregone conclusion."

Sometimes, to be sure, arbitrary premises are accepted "for the sake of argument" and the conclusion is discounted accordingly. Premises founded on fact are necessary, however, to prove a point seriously. Sometimes we wish to avoid the job of getting the facts together and weighing them, so we state an assumption, *taking it for granted* there is no disagreement. We may introduce it with a strong leading phrase like:

Everybody knows . . .
Unquestionably . . .
It is only too clear . . .
You can't deny that . . .
It goes without saying . . .
All intelligent persons agree . . . (An especially mean one, for if you don't agree you are stupid.)

When you hear one of these tom-toms be on guard; a "self-evident truth" may be lurking just around the corner.

The artist Lichty, in one of his popular "Grin and Bear It" cartoons, pictures a trembling college professor under investigation by a Senate Committee. The stern chairman wags a long forefinger under the witness's nose:

"You agree that professors are *absent-minded,* Professor?. . .

"Then you admit you absent-mindedly might have overthrown the government at some time or other!"

The renowned historian Lord Macaulay was very sure of himself. He would often preface an assertion with the words, "Every schoolboy knows." An unkind critic undertook to collect the information in the skull of this remarkable schoolboy, and found it would fill a tidy-sized encyclopedia. Imitating the noble lord's method, a citizen in Brooklyn concludes an angry letter to the New York *Herald Tribune* about an involved interpretation of the Bill of Rights with the words: "A fact known to every school child." Maybe the youngsters now are all versed in constitutional law, but not in my day.

Here is a gentleman vigorously arguing that there is life after death. When his opponent demands how he knows it, he replies: "Because it was never the intention of the Creator that it should be otherwise." In effect, he has presumed to enter into the Creator's mind.

"True Christians act thus and so," "Real patriots do such and such," are warning signals. The speaker assumes it as self-evident that what *he* means by a "Christian," or a "patriot," is the only true meaning. If he happens to be a powerful demagogue trying to monopolize the definition of patriotism, citizens who oppose him are in for trouble.

FIFTH AMENDMENT

"Fifth Amendment Communist" is a glaring example of the fallacy. A witness before an investigating committee refuses to answer a question, pleading the protection of the Fifth Amendment to the Constitution. The Amendment stipulates that a person does not have to testify against himself, and that he may not "be deprived of life, liberty or property without due process of law."

The witness makes the appeal because his lawyer tells him to, or because he is actually a member of the Party, or because he does not want to implicate innocent friends. Whatever the reason, good or bad, usually no competent evidence of criminal activities has been found against him. He has had no proper trial, with proper rules of evidence. Yet by refusing to answer the question he stands condemned in the eyes of the committee, and of the public, as a Communist— a "Fifth Amendment Communist." An inference is drawn about his motives, so strong it seems "self-evident." But "self-evidence" is not legal evidence and when constitutional rights are denied to anyone, even a criminal or a subversive, they are weakened for everybody else. The U.S. Supreme Court, in its decision of April 9, 1956, has this to say:

We must condemn the practice of imputing a sinister meaning to the exercise of a person's constitutional right under the Fifth Amendment. The privilege against self-incrimination would be reduced to a hollow mockery if its exercise could be taken as equivalent either to a confession of guilt or a conclusive presumption of perjury.

This is not to say that the witness should or should not plead the Fifth Amendment. (Personally I feel that he usually should not.) This is only to point out that the witness has been "proved" to be a Communist not by the facts, but by a "self-evident truth." If a prosecutor should rise up in a court of law and say: "Your Honor, everyone knows that the defendant is guilty of a monstrous crime!" he would not get beyond the first four words.

WHAT EVERYBODY KNOWS

A St. Louis newspaperman, assigned to the Office of Air Surgeon during World War II, met Dr. K., an authority on physical therapy, and inquired: "Dr. K., why do athletes, particularly those who have gone into strenuous professional games such as football, always die young?"

"You have proof of this statement?" asked the doctor.

"Everybody knows that it is true; you read about it in the papers all the time."

"Young man, there are a number of large books written on this subject. I am probably the only man who has read them all. Each disagrees with the other, but now you tell me everybody knows!"

"Well—er—what I really meant was, it is my opinion that professional athletes die young."

"Ah," said Dr. K., "that is your *opinion*! Good. With opinions I will not spend my time arguing."

What "everybody knows" would fill many tidy-sized encyclopedias. Today everybody knows that the earth goes round the sun in 365¼ days—at least in the West we know it. But five hundred years ago everybody "knew" the opposite—that the sun moves across the sky while the earth stands still.

Many well-worn sayings and proverbs are widely accepted as proof of a statement.[1] Not only is it assumed that no facts are required, but often the saying contradicts modern knowledge. "Nobody works unless he has to," is as firmly believed as it is psychologically unsound. The human anatomy and nervous system are adapted for work—which does not mean that people enjoy every variety of work—for instance tightening up nut number 16 on an assembly line all day long.

[1] We are getting close to *ad populum*, appeal to the crowd, developed in Chapter 13.

"Women can't understand public questions" will probably survive long after the League of Women Voters has made the average female voter better informed than the male.

> Fright can turn your hair white overnight.
> Nothing succeeds like success.
> A miss is as good as a mile.
> Genius is the infinite capacity for taking pains.
> Spare the rod and spoil the child.
> Time is money.

It is very difficult to prove any of these common sayings. "The exception proves the rule" is a useful club to have handy, for it provides an out in any argument. If your opponent comes up with some facts you can't get around, you accept them, saying, "Yes indeed, but doesn't the exception prove the rule?" That is, your rule. It is interesting to remember that the proverb has two meanings. In the original one "prove" meant to *test*— which makes sense. "The exception tests the validity of the rule."

The *Reader's Digest* (October, 1934) collected pairs of proverbs which flatly contradicted one another, such as:

> "Look before you leap." *But*
> "He who hesitates is lost."

> "Leave well enough alone." *But*
> "Progress never stands still."

> "A man gets no more than he pays for." *But*
> "The best things in life are free."

Proverbs and adages, like old shoes, are comfortable and easy. They help keep the conversation going and sometimes reflect real wisdom. But they should never be accepted in lieu of solid proof.

Self-evident truths, more perhaps than any other fallacy,

tend to come up from the unconscious. They are usually rooted in culture and language, the way our minds learned to work before we were old enough to remember. Thus they vary greatly around the world. In the American culture it is self-evident that the death of a normal young person is tragic. Other cultures have a different attitude. Mexicans, for instance, say *"es mejor con Dios."* "He is better off with God."

Morris Cohen observes that self-evident truth might equally well be called intuition. "Very few men in the history of philosophy," he says, "have been able to resist at all times the lure of intuitively revealed truth." Thus all the early astronomers, including Copernicus, believed that the orbits of the planets were circular. They felt in their bones that any self-respecting planet had to travel in a perfect circle.

It is difficult, says Cohen, to find a proposition for which self-evidence has never been claimed. For the greater part of human history it was self-evident that the world was flat. It was similarly obvious that water could never run uphill, until the discovery of the siphon proved otherwise.

BY DEFINITION

In a variation of the fallacy, a proposition is sometimes declared valid "by definition." In 1951 Red China's General Wu appeared before the Assembly of the United Nations to deny that China was an aggressor in Korea.

"It cannot possibly be so," he said.

"Why not?" he was asked.

"Because my government, *by definition*, is a peace-loving nation."

Meanwhile a typical piece of Moscow logic takes the form:

"Russia has freedom, America has none."

"What's that again?"

"Capitalism, *by definition*, enslaves the workers."
This would be news to members of the AF of L-CIO.

Propositions which are "self-evident," or established by definition, must undergo a rigorous test before we are justified in using them. They may look convincing because they are so familiar, but we will do well to turn them over on their backs and look again.

16
Black or White

Fallacy Number Twelve

THE MODERATOR of a famous radio debate program used to hold up a ball and ask the studio audience what color it was. When they answered "white," he would turn the ball around and ask again. "Black," they would say. Then he would point the moral; every question has two sides and we should listen to both. But, as Mr. Leo Cherne objects in a discussion of radio debates, the big issues today are no longer merely black or white, if indeed they ever were.[1] They have many sides, not just two sides, and we must allow for shades of gray.

Classical logicians, like debaters, tend to take the absolute position, impatient of in-between relationships. They like things open or shut, true or false, good or bad, right or wrong. This may give them the mental satisfaction of a tidy paper solution, but it does not help them understand their world. Whenever we force a problem which contains shades of gray into an unyielding pattern of black and white, we distort the solution and hamper our own understanding.

John and Mary are being divorced. Their friends line up in two hostile camps. One group declares that it is all *his* fault, the other that it is *her* fault. Quite possibly the fault lies with neither. Forces beyond the control of John and Mary may be causing them to separate. Their education or habits or religion may be sharply antagonistic. They may even possess

[1] *New York Times* Magazine, March 2, 1952.

incompatible blood types which prevent them from having children. For most broken marriages there is a process involved, a spiral of many causes. It is unreasonable to insist on a rigid one-cause-and-effect interpretation, with somebody exclusively to blame.

"Women are bad drivers!" says Mr. Roe, contemplating another bill for a crumpled fender. "You're wrong," cries his friend Doe, "women are good drivers, better than men!" And off they go, hammer and tongs. What are the facts? Records of accidents indicate that in some respects women drivers do better than men, in other respects worse, and two-valued reasoning over-simplifies the question. Women disorganize more fenders and bumpers, but have fewer crashes involving personal injury. Supporting evidence is found in lower insurance rates for women in some states.

MANY SITUATIONS ARE TWO-VALUED

In the early spring of 1955 I heard a man say: "It's either the Yankees or the Red Sox in the American League"—thereby shrinking an eight-valued question into two, before a ball had been pitched. But when in late September the pennants were clinched in both major leagues, a real two-valued choice appeared: Either the New York Yankees or the Brooklyn Dodgers would win the World Series. Plenty of pertinent discussion was in order, and the opportunity, as I remember it, was not neglected.

Many factual situations are legitimately two-valued. The electric current is either on or off, as every householder knows. When the trigger is pulled, the gun goes off or it doesn't. The car won't run or it will—though sometimes in fits and starts. The lady who said she was "only a little bit pregnant" had no case. Our task is to determine which situations are really two-valued, and which are multi-valued.

DEEP IN THE LANGUAGE

A major reason for black-or-white thinking is the structure of the English language, indeed, linguists say, of all the Indo-European languages, including Sanscrit, Greek, and Latin, as well as modern European tongues. Children speaking these languages are brought up to think in *opposites*—little vs. big, long vs. short, clean vs. dirty, hero vs. villain, love vs. hate, good vs. bad, life vs. death. It takes a real effort to break out of this linguistic conditioning.

Other languages do not have this hard and fast dichotomy, so that for their speakers the multi-valued approach is easier. A Chinese, for instance, says: "The long and the short are mutually related"; "the hard and the easy are mutually complementary"; "the front and the rear mutually accompany each other."[2] It is possible that the Marxists are going to have a lot of trouble forcing the two-valued notion of a choice between Capitalism or Communism on the Chinese rank and file. Russians accept it readily, as Russian is an Indo-European language.

Not only our language but our habits make Americans think this way. Living under pressure we feel that we must decide things fast. "Make up your mind, Mac!" We skip lightly to inferences and value judgments in order to come to the point of action—where indeed the situation may be a yes-or-no choice, often an irrevocable one, as in pulling a trigger. For many Americans it seems easier to act than to think, and when we do think, we like to make it fast. Our comic books and TV dramas feed our appetite for rapid action.

John Steinbeck, writing in the *Reporter*, described how his young son, Catbird, learned to tell the Good Guys from the Bad Guys in TV horse opera. It's simple, said Catbird, the Good Guy wears a white hat and the Bad Guy a black hat. The

---

[2] Chang Tung-sun in *ETC.*, Spring, 1952.

Good Guy is clean-shaven, the Bad Guy has dark stubble on his chin. Sometimes, said Catbird, there is an In-Between Guy in a gray hat, but he doesn't last. If he starts bad he ends good, and if he starts good he ends bad. The *Reporter* proceeds to editorialize: "Catbird's simple formula is attractive, but before long he will surely discover that it's not so simple to divide the world's cast of characters into Good Guys and Bad Guys, that black-and-white judgments need tempering, and that even the grays are deceptive."

But Washington, according to James Reston, keeps right on dividing the Good Guys from the Bad.[3] "Congress," he says, "is now dividing for and against John Foster Dulles, Secretary of State, and the main question, about the President's foreign policy decisions in the Korean, Formosan and Indo-China crises, is getting lost." The big issues were buried in a wrangle as to whether Mr. Dulles was right or wrong in his "brink of war" interview in *Life* magazine.

The case of Marriner Eccles, sometime Chairman of the Federal Reserve Board, is also instructive. During the depression of the 1930's he was known as a "spender," a disciple of Lord Keynes. With full employment and creeping inflation after the war, Eccles called for rigorous economy in government. Many financial experts could not believe their ears, for how could a "spender" preach economy? Once a spender, they reasoned, always a spender. But sound fiscal policy must be flexible, and the Keynes theory supports Mr. Eccles: spend in the downswings, save and pay off the debt in the upswings.

SCIENCE IS MULTI-VALUED

Scientists, who take no conclusions for granted, come up from time to time with borderline cases that destroy a familiar, sharp division. When Frederick Wöhler synthesized urea in

[3] *New York Times*, January 24, 1956.

his laboratory in 1828, chemists at first refused to credit it. They had been taught to believe that "organic" and "inorganic" substances were forever different. But Wöhler broke out of the Aristotelian strait jacket, boldly took inorganic materials, and made them behave like the organic compound urea. This in effect turned a two-valued situation into a many-valued one and opened new vistas to science. The chemists, in the face of a laboratory demonstration which they themselves could repeat, gradually recovered from their shock, to the great advantage of the progress of chemistry.

Living things are still verbally classified as either "animal" or "vegetable," but this hard-and-fast distinction no longer holds for biologists. Here is Euglena, which digests food like an animal, and employs photosynthesis like a plant. Here are the Ascidians, usually classed as animals, but they produce cellulose, a unique function of plants.

For centuries medical men made a sharp distinction between mind and body. Today most of them accept the idea of psychosomatic medicine, where mind and body are treated as parts of one organism, the total man. It is now admitted that too much worry (psychic) about his balance sheet can give a big executive stomach ulcers (somatic); while too many strawberry sundaes (somatic) may cause Jackie to flunk his history exam (psychic). The mental healing of certain cases of physical illness is an established fact, but the attempt to cure *every* lesion by this means gives us yet another unfortunate example of two-valued thinking.

In 1953, Dr. Elizabeth Forbes-Sempill, forty years old, daughter of the late Lord Sempill, went into a private hospital for an operation, presently to emerge as Dr. Ewan Forbes-Sempill. She was no longer "female" but "male," and in line for the family title and estates. Dr. Elizabeth is only one case in many where modern surgery has reversed the supposedly irreversible fact of one's sex.

Fluorine is now the subject of a bitter two-valued debate. It is of course a *poison* in any considerable dose. But one part to a million in drinking water protects children's teeth against decay, and no deleterious effects have been detected. Certain towns in the West for years have been safely drinking local water containing up to thirty parts in a million. Many citizens apparently are reasoning, however, "fluorine is either a poison or it is not. If it is, we don't want any part of it in our drinking water." They are blocking adoption, and their children, one fears, are going to pay a heavy price for this exercise in bad logic.

You are either dead or alive—but are you? Here is Harry A. Jones, sixty-six, of Long Beach, California.[4] He was found by his wife slumped over his desk, and the doctor she summoned could find "no pulse, no heart beat nor any sign of breath." He was pronounced dead, and a hearse was called to take him to the mortuary. On the road, the blankets covering him began to move, causing the driver of the hearse a very bad moment. Mr. Jones happily "came back to life, and the astonished doctors at Long Beach Veterans Hospital said he was making a remarkable recovery."

ZONING AGAIN

Our town held a zoning hearing to discuss whether a man should be permitted to open a toy shop in an area zoned for residences. Arguments flew back and forth, each a little more general and a little more heated than the last, until an all-out battle began to rage between those who held that "little business" was good for rural towns, and those who were positive it was bad—a strictly black-or-white battle. The questions of

[4] AP dispatch, September 11, 1954.

what particular kind of business, the possible hardship to the
applicant, the force of the zoning code already adopted—all
were forgotten in the mighty hassle. The debate, stimulating
as it was to the contestants, became meaningless so far as the
problem in hand was concerned. Members of the Board who
hoped to benefit by the hearing were only further confused.

Later, however, when the Board met in executive session,
it had to make a two-valued decision—whether to allow the
toy shop or deny it.[5] Many variables had to be considered for
which the public hearing contributed almost nothing.

Local communities constantly run into similar discussions,
discussions that are meaningless until they are pulled down to
earth. You have heard plenty of them:

Private schools vs. public schools.
City living vs. country living.
Chemical fertilizers vs. good old barn manure. (This one can
get very bitter indeed, with manure usually way ahead on a
decibel count.)
Science vs. religion.
Freedom vs. regimentation.

The last argument has been around for a long time. One side
in the debate says we must have complete freedom or submit
to slavery. But a philosopher saw the fallacy when he observed:
"Your freedom to swing your arms ends where my nose begins." Freedom is always relative: freedom to do what? Using
the two-valued approach in a situation that has many values is
like stepping into a shower bath without a mixer, a stream
which runs either scalding hot or freezing cold.

John Doe and Richard Roe are arguing about the respective
places of Truman and Eisenhower in history. "Truman contained Russia with the Marshall Plan, to his eternal credit!"
says Doe. "Eisenhower stopped the Korean War, to his eternal

[5] The Board denied

credit!" says Roe. . . . And so on, with steadily rising voices. To the listener, it soon appears that the argument is so two-valued for each contestant that their minds can never meet. There is a simple way to test this—provided the listener can get the floor. He asks John Doe: "Did Truman ever do anything wrong?" "No!" exclaims Doe. The listener turns to Roe. "Did Truman ever do anything right?" Another "No!" is clear proof that the situation is beyond human aid.

ARYANS AND NON-ARYANS

Hitler, like all fanatics and demagogues, preferred to operate in terms of black or white. He divided humanity into Aryans (good) and non-Aryans (bad). Then he proceeded to examine a great variety of things on the same basis. Is this piece of music Aryan or non-Aryan? If the latter, put the composer in a concentration camp! Is this painting Aryan? Does this book, this piece of architecture, this mathematics, physics, religion, system of calisthenics, cookery, conform to Aryanism? The Japanese, as valuable allies to Germany, posed a nice logical problem. Obviously they were "good," but also by no stretch of the imagination could they be classed as members of the Aryan race. The tough problem was solved by giving them the special designation of "non-non-Aryans." Ultimately it covered quite a group of allies.

The Russian Communists have had similar difficulties with their music, theater, ballet, novels, poetry, painting, women's clothes, science, and practically everything else. Conclaves of scientists have solemnly met in Moscow to decide what was "Marxian physics" and what was not. The Lysenko controversy about the principles of genetics was a strictly two-valued row.

In Moscow, everything the regime considers good is labeled "Communistic," everything bad is "capitalistic"; very little is in-between. Such thinking is characteristic of totalitarian regimes, which to stay in power must make sharp, police-court distinctions between friends and enemies. A man who says "a plague on both your houses" goes to Siberia. Reinhold Neibuhr sums it up:[6]

Lenin did not, of course, originate the fanaticism that was inherent in the whole Marxist dogma, with its too simple distinctions between exploited and exploiter, its too-simple conception of the close structure of society, its too-simple derivation of all social evil from the institution of property, and its consequent division of the whole world into friends and enemies "of the people." Stalin boasted considerable flexibility . . . but it never dissolved the fanaticism. Thus, we could be allies of the Russians during the war, but it was not long before . . . the world was sharply divided once more into the hosts of good and evil.

REVERSE TWIST

Stalin and Hitler had no monopoly on totalitarian logic. It is incipient in every community where a leader strives for absolute power. Eternal vigilance is the price of political freedom. After World War II, when Americans relaxed this vigilance, certain demagogues managed to capture the headlines with arguments that not only divided the world into black and white nations (very few were white), but divided all U.S. citizens into either Communist sympathizers or "patriots." McCarthy's followers insisted that anyone who criticized the Senator was a Communist, or at best a fellow traveler.[7] Such reasoning turns an honest difference of opinion into a criminal charge, and can fill the land with fear and conflict.

After Bishop Sheil of Chicago criticized McCarthy in 1954,

[6] *New Leader,* October 3, 1955.
[7] This is also a circular argument. "Mr. X. is a Communist." "How do you know?" "Because he disagrees with me." "Why does he disagree with you?" "Because I am against Communism."

letters bristling with black-or-white choices began to appear in the papers, reading like this:[8]

> Destroy all Communists in America—it's either them or us!
>
> I am aware that some highly respected personalities have joined in the attack on McCarthy, but in my book, regardless of their big names, anyone who seeks to discredit McCarthy is sympathetic to the Reds.
>
> Say! Whose side are you on anyway?
>
> The attack on McCarthy is the front line of a continuing attack on the U.S. Congress which will end only in the destruction of the Communists or of the Congress.

A curious by-product appeared as demagogic voices grew more shrill. For a time it seemed that loyal citizens who dared not attempt a direct challenge were increasingly forced to take the *opposite* of every position assumed by Moscow. If Moscow advocates disarmament, we must oppose it; if Moscow is for peace, we must be for war; if Moscow demands economic aid to backward countries, we must be against it. In effect, such citizens were bound fast to the foreign policy of the Kremlin, leaving American policy no room in which to maneuver! Republicans and Democrats suffer from a similar obsession. When one party introduces a good bill in Congress, members of the other party feel bound to oppose it.

WE OR THEY

This brings us to the number one question threatening our planet—how to avoid World War III. For the present the belligerents are observing a thermonuclear truce, but the stockpiles are growing day by day in East and West. To avoid ultimate explosion, negotiation on various levels must be attempted—everything from joint weather stations to disarma-

---

[8] Actual quotations from these letters. The last one is also a thin-entering-wedge case.

ment proposals. But how can negotiation be seriously considered, much less experimented with, if the East stubbornly insists that it cannot live in the same world with "capitalism," and the West stubbornly insists that it cannot live in the same world with "Communism"? C. L. Sulzberger, after a long interview with Molotov, reported that "Moscow continues to view the two systems as incompatible, as implacably hostile. There is no third or middle way."[9]

HOMEWORK

A lot of us, however, lock ourselves up whenever such issues are before the house. Here is the front page of the *New York Times* for March 18, 1956. There are at least three headline stories which can be, and are, reduced to black-or-white reasoning. I will give the exact headline, and then my comments.

"TRUMAN ASSAILS GOP ASSERTION REDS ARE LOSING"

Reds are *either* gaining (Truman), *or* losing (Dulles). A terrific battle is in progress over Dulles' statement that the U.S. is in a stronger position, vis-à-vis Russia, in early 1956 than it was in early 1955. The arguers talk as if they were viewing a prize fight, and discussing who is ahead on points. Actually, of course, the Soviets are gaining in some places—as in the Middle East, and losing in other places—as in Germany, with the creation of the new German Army. Where the balance lies, nobody really knows, and it would take a large university staff to find out.

"ELLENDER WARNS SOUTH ON FORCE"

The Senator's warning is wise, but his logic takes the form: *either* peaceful and strong protest, *or* back to the days of

[9] *New York Times*, January 14, 1956.

reconstruction and the carpetbaggers. It is not so simple, Senator. The South of 1956 is not the South of 1866. Her economy is vastly different, with industrial penetration everywhere; relations with the North are very different; and above all the Negro population is now almost a hundred years away from slavery. Violence by Southerners may bring catastrophe, but it will not be that of reconstruction days.

"FRENCH AGAIN ADD TO ALGERIAN FORCE"

Algeria must *either* be free, *or* be enslaved by France—such seems to be the logic of the Algerian nationalists. Again too simple; it does not allow for more than a million Frenchmen living in Algeria, and for other profound complications.

Any front page on almost any day can give us similar homework in finding shades of gray.

17

Guilt by Association

Fallacy Number Thirteen

GUILT by association rests on the classicists' first Law of Thought, A is A. The fallacy arises when unlike things are equated and the identification is spurious. The words may be the same, but the things behind the words are not.

Few people distinguish between equality and identity. A half dollar and five dimes are equal but they are not identical. Even two half dollars are not identical, and semanticists quarrel with the classical corollary: "A thing is always equal to itself." They say this ignores the time factor. Most objects or events represent a changing process through time—an apple, for instance, or even a mountain.

The fallacy we are discussing is more obvious, however. It equates unlike entities on the basis of a single common trait. Without this brand of crippled thinking, the phenomenon known as "McCarthyism"[1] could hardly have gained a foothold. Here is an example that shows the lengths to which the reasoning may be pushed:

In 1954, Senator Ralph Flanders severely criticized Senator McCarthy on the Senate floor, rousing the latter's followers to a blistering counterattack. Flanders expected that a certain

---

[1] "McCarthyism. 1. public accusation of disloyalty, especially of pro-Communist activity, in many instances unsupported by proof, or based on slight, doubtful or irrelevant evidence." *American College Dictionary*, 1955.

charge would be brought against him, and he anticipated it by a statement to the press: It is true, he said, that "a brother of the wife of Alger Hiss is my brother's wife's sister's divorced husband." Hiss, convicted in court of perjury and serving a prison term at the time, was the number one symbol of Communist subversion.

Flanders' statement is complicated but we can help decipher it by assigning common names to his relatives; thus:

Senator Flanders has a brother we will call "John."

"John" has a wife we will call "Susan."

"Susan" has a sister we will call "Dorothy."

"Dorothy" was married to a man we will call "Walter"—but she divorced him.

"Walter" is the brother of Priscilla (this is her real name).

Priscilla is the wife of Alger Hiss.

Therefore Senator Flanders would probably have been "proved" a darling of the Kremlin, if he had not forestalled the charge with his statement. Assisted by this fallacy the taint of Communism might readily seep through these various relatives until it stained the Senator himself.

DEFINITIONS

"Guilt by association" is an omnibus term which needs some breaking down. It covers:

1. *Physical association* where the accused is repeatedly seen in close company with known public enemies, thus warranting suspicion of contamination.

2. *Physical association* where the accused is obviously uncontaminated. Winston Churchill was seen in the company of Joseph Stalin during various war conferences, but nobody outside a mental hospital ever accused Churchill of being a Stalinite.

3. *Association by kinship*—as in the Flanders case. No sub-

versive acts are charged—only that the person is related to an alleged subversive. This is strongly reminiscent of certain alarming practices of the Inquisition. The "heretic" was the victim then, and Protestants were convicted by the ecclesiastical courts and given horrible punishments on the grounds of guilt by kinship. "The beliefs of relatives," says Eleanor Bontecou,[2] "were held to be presumptive proof of the guilt of the accused. In one case, the charge against a man was that his mother was a heretic, that she often used to visit him, and sometimes helped him when he was in need." The charge, if not the punishment, can be matched today. In 1955, a series of officers in the armed services were discharged or denied commissions because of the alleged beliefs of their relatives.[3] They included W. K. Novak of the Army and Eugene Landy of the Navy, both of whose mothers had had leftist connections in the past.

4. *Guilt by verbal association*, where no physical association is necessarily involved at all. The accusation is based on a characteristic of the person similar to a characteristic of an alleged public enemy. It is the most frequent form of the fallacy and the one with which I am chiefly concerned in this chapter.

5. *Innocence by association*, the reverse of the above, which can be equally fallacious. The accused defends himself by listing various important and respectable people who are his friends. The late Judge Woolsey gave us a dramatic warning: "Before judging a man by his associates, remember that Judas Iscariot traveled in the best of company "

In his campaign for the Senate in 1954, Richard Neuberger of Oregon was under constant attack on the guilt-by-associa-

---

[2] *The Federal Loyalty Security Program* (Cornell University Press, 1953).

[3] After public opinion had been aroused, some of these officers were reinstated.

tion formula. One charge was that he wrote for "leftist" magazines like the *Nation*. He also wrote for conservative magazines like the *Saturday Evening Post*, but this was not mentioned by his opponents. Said the Senator:

I can write for a radical magazine without being a radical, a conservative magazine without being a conservative, a Canadian magazine without transferring my citizenship, a woman's magazine without being a woman.

You can indeed, Senator, but if your political opponent thinks that there is still mileage in the fallacy, he will dismiss any such reasonable interpretation.

If we can keep our eyes on *specific acts*, we need never be lost in this verbal no-man's land. What crime did the accused commit? Had he access to military secrets? Did he hide machine guns against "the revolution"? What papers did he hand over to a Russian spy?

THE WORDS ARE THE SAME, THEREFORE

Guilt by verbal association can perhaps best be clarified by a famous case, with a false syllogism which illuminates the trick involved. The case has been widely quoted, to the point oí becoming a classic.

The late Senator Robert A. Taft did not hesitate to express what he thought was right, even when it did not harmonize with Republican ideology. In the great housing shortage after World War II, he concluded that some public housing was necessary, and he co-operated in introducing the Wagner-Ellender-Taft housing bill. He qualified his support by suggesting that public housing be limited to 10 percent of the people in the lowest income brackets.

The National Association of Real Estate Boards was opposed to public housing in any form, however limited, and vigorously fought the bill. The executive vice-president of the Association was quoted as saying that to the extent Senator Taft supports the bill "he shares in the philosophies of Socialism, Communism and Fascism. It will lick the pants off him if he goes for it." At another time, the real estate executive is said to have declared that the Senator was "lined up with Communism." The press carried these attacks widely, for newspapers love a fight. Let us reduce them to a syllogism:

> All Communists favor public housing.
> Senator Taft favors public housing.
> Therefore Senator Taft is a Communist.

Things equal to the same thing are equal to each other. But are they? We will now construct another syllogism:

> All Communists have a blood temperature of 98.6 degrees (except when thinking about Wall Street).
> Senator Taft has a blood temperature of 98.6 degrees (except when thinking about the New Deal).
> Therefore Senator Taft is a Communist.

We can all see what is wrong with the second syllogism, but many Americans were confused by the first—though the logic is precisely the same. The trick is to find one characteristic, just one, which your man shares with a public enemy, and then leap to the conclusion that other characteristics are interchangeable. As everyone has thousands of characteristics —height, weight, age, sex, race, eye color, blood temperature, religion, occupation, political beliefs, attitudes, opinions, and so endlessly onward—it is child's play to find a common one between any two people, or between a person and an organization. If you need suggestions, Raymond Cattell once prepared an alphabetical list of 171 personal attributes, beginning with *acquisitive, alert, alcoholic*—and ending no doubt with *zealous* and *zestful*.

With some common bond established, such as advocacy of public housing, or contributions to a given charity, guilt can be "proved," well enough at least to make the headlines, and cause many citizens to shake their heads in honest bewilderment. It sounds ridiculous when the trick is exposed. It *is* ridiculous, but hundreds of loyal Americans have suffered because of it. Some of them have been financially ruined, more than one has committed suicide, the morale of the State Department has been badly damaged, the Voice of America reduced to a shambles, and the nation split into angry factions. With this logical meat ax it is possible to "prove" anybody guilty of anything.

> The Pope favors child labor laws.
> The Politburo favors child labor laws.
> Therefore the Pope is a Communist, or
> Therefore the Politburo is Catholic.

It may work either way, you see.

Does the alert reader think he is immune? Just sit right there while the investigator asks you a few questions. You went to Harvard, did you not? That is unfortunate, most unfortunate. Senator McCarthy carried on a bitter vendetta against intellectuals in general and Harvard in particular, calling it a hotbed of subversion and a "smelly mess." Several of his victims were members of the Harvard faculty. So how could you, a Harvard man, escape contamination? . . . What, you were in college *before* those professors were apprehended? But how could the professors have gained a foothold unless the ground had been prepared—answer me that? Harvard must have been Red all along to tolerate Reds. You admit that, don't you? And speaking of Reds, where did those crimson colors come from? You don't know? I'll give you just ten minutes to find out!

> Many subversives went to Harvard.
> The reader went to Harvard.
> Therefore the reader is subversive.

A similar line of reasoning can be applied to practically any association or connection or family relationship you ever had, to every word you ever wrote, and every book you ever read. David Lilienthal was charged with Communism on the Senate floor because his parents came from Czecho-Slovakia in the 1880's, more than fifty years before it became a "satellite.", Guilt can seep through kinfolk not only in the present, but half a century into the past.

FORMAL LOGIC SAYS NO

Aristotle's formal logic does not allow the syllogisms arranged above about Senator Taft, the Pope, and the Harvard man. A formal syllogism has only three terms, as noted earlier, and should use some form of the verb *to be*. To make a correct syllogism out of the Taft housing case it might read:

Only Communists are in favor of public housing.
Senator Taft is in favor of public housing.
Therefore Senator Taft is a Communist.

Here the first premise is obviously false to the facts and gives the case away. Or it might read:

All Communists are in favor of public housing.
Senator Taft is a Communist.
Therefore Senator Taft is in favor of public housing.

Here *Communist* is the proper middle term, which must be "distributed" or generalized in one premise, then must disappear in the conclusion. If the real estate boards had used this classic form, which demands that Senator Taft be labeled a Communist in the *premise* rather than in the conclusion, it is probable that the publicity balloon would never have got off the ground. The formal syllogism, you see, has its uses.

STAIRCASE OF GUILT

Charges of guilt by association can be arranged in a series of steps, each more remote from the starting point.

On the basement floor is Mr. X., *a member of the U.S. Communist party today* (the date is important), and so in effect an agent of a foreign power, and a potential spy or saboteur. He needs diligent watching by the FBI.

On the first step above stand Communist *fellow travelers*. If it can be proved that they follow the Moscow line, shifting as it shifts, they are suspects too.

The next step takes us to those *old-line Marxists* who are at war with Moscow and the American Communist party. They are for "the revolution" all right, but they are *not* agents of a foreign power. Furthermore, they are not a menace so long as the country keeps reasonably prosperous. Only if we have twenty million unemployed will they begin to attract a following.

Then come the *Socialists*, who advocate peaceful change without revolution. Norman Thomas leads this contingent, now much decimated, and he is no more an agent of a foreign power than Bernard Baruch.

On the next higher step we find *New Dealers*. They too are a dwindling company in 1956—but critics pursue them with false syllogisms:

New Dealers favor public power.
Socialists favor public power.
Therefore the New Deal is Creeping Socialism.

This shoe, however, will fit the other foot:

Republican governors (in the far western states) favor public power.
Socialists favor public power.[4]
Therefore Republican governors are Socialists.

[4] The liberals sometimes throw false syllogisms back at the conservatives:
    Hitler worked closely with Big Business.
    The Steel Corporation is Big Business.
    Therefore the Steel Corporation is lined up with Fascism.

Up another step are *reformers and liberals* of all shades, often called "parlor pinks" on Capitol Hill, and by definition "soft toward Communism." Advocates of racial and religious tolerance are found here, likely to be branded as stooges of the Kremlin by anti-Semites. As for agnostics, atheists, and other dissenters, they are of course held to be followers of Lenin, who once said that religion was "the opiate of the people."

On the next step are *supporters of the United Nations*. The fact that President Eisenhower is pledged to the UN offers them scant protection. In Southern California it is said to be less dangerous to be found studying the *Communist Manifesto* than defending UNESCO. "Internationalism and Communism are Siamese twins and the synonym is treason."[5]

The final step in the staircase leads to *anyone with ideas*. During the great days of McCarthyism, just to use your mind intelligently could readily identify you with "Communist-type thinking."

Charges of treason and subversion have been briskly transferred up and down this staircase, on the principle of verbal association. Citizens at any step could be equated with the real subversives on the ground floor. The calumny was fluid, flexible, and mostly beyond legal reach. General of the Army George Marshall, as well as Senator Taft, was called an agent of the Kremlin. One Congressional Committee tried to subpoena President Truman to answer to the implied charge of treason—did he or did he not once have contact with Harry Dexter White? Some citizens from the South have hinted at subversion in the U.S. Supreme Court because of its anti-segregation rulings.

[5] Letter to the New York *Herald Tribune*, February, 1954.

Communists are opposed to segregation.
The Supreme Court is opposed to segregation.
Therefore the Court is following the Communist line.

Very few Americans can define a Communist. I have roughly
defined them above in the first three steps of the staircase:
Party members today, fellow travelers today, and old-line
Marxists. Dr. Samuel Stouffer, in an article in *Look* which
summarizes a large project in opinion research, has this to say
about the persons interviewed, a sample carefully chosen to
represent all adult Americans:

When they were asked what they thought Communists were,
many of them seemed to use the term simply as a convenient
synonym for "that which I dislike or distrust": e.g., non-religious
people, supporters of the United Nations, intellectuals, ardent
advocates of peace, etc.—in other words, non-conformists.

All of which puts us in mind of the man who was making
a serious disturbance at a May Day parade in New York. When
a policeman tried to silence him the man protested: "But,
officer, I'm an anti-Communist!"

"I don't care what kind of Communist you are, get outa
here!"

18
Town Meeting

WE HAVE worked our way, with many examples, through thirteen fallacies. Some of them are lapses not so much in logic as in fact-finding, often through accepting unwarranted assumptions. If one assumes that the moon is made of green cheese, it is logical to conclude that the first space ship from the earth need not stock so many provisions. The trouble is with the assumption. The trouble with reasoning in a circle is that the conclusion is planted in the premise and no true logical process takes place at all.

Certainly all the thirteen are impediments to straight thinking, road blocks that throw us off the track and detour our reasoning powers. Some of the patterns, we remember, have their legitimate uses—analogy, for instance, and generalizing—and these call for extra care. Others can produce jokes and wisecracks, such as Irish bulls, and the policeman story which ended the last chapter.

A *post hoc* is always suspect, but taking the trouble to analyze and correct it may establish valuable new knowledge. The first *post hoc* argument connecting lung cancer and cigarette smoking proved nothing in itself, but it sparked a number of important scientific investigations. There is nothing wrong with generalizing or with extrapolation as such; human living, to say nothing of scientific progress, demands both. It is when the facts are too few to warrant a generalization, or the points on the curve inadequate to warrant even a cautious ride into the future, that the fallacies arise.

Suppose we try an experiment in which a single question is asked, to be answered thirteen different ways, each illustrating one of the fallacies. If the reader is like the author, something of the sort is now required. After many pages of description, one needs—at least I need when reading somebody else's book—a summary, as well as a reminder system with which to recall the main points and distinctions.

The reader can hardly have failed to note my interest in local zoning. Again and again while writing this book, I have been called from my desk to attend meetings of the Zoning Board of Appeals of my town (population three thousand), to officiate at public hearings, to inspect properties whose owners had applied for "variances," or exceptions to the zoning regulations. In the course of this civic duty I have heard countless arguments, supported by all known varieties of logic, good, bad, and indifferent. As a member of the Board of Appeals I have fancied myself a kind of grass-roots judge, and have tried to be especially conscientious in weighing evidence, checking assumptions, separating rumor from fact.

What I propose to do, accordingly, is to illustrate each of the thirteen fallacies by a reply to the question: *"Should our town adopt zoning?"* The replies will all be in the negative, and will begin with an emphatic "No! because—"

I cannot say that I have personally heard every reply precisely as given, but I have heard most of them, and the rest come from reports of other towns.[1] If zoning bores the reader, let him think of some local matter which does not bore him —his schools, the volunteer fire department, traffic control, jury service, service club, board of directors. He is sure to find most of the thirteen there too. Note that the answers illustrate both honest confusion and eagerness to make a case against the proposal.

[1] The *Connecticut State Journal*, for instance, in July, 1955, collected a series of ferocious anti-zoning arguments from the town of Southington.

I have also added a well-worn example of each fallacy, taken from earlier chapters, as a tickler.

1. OVER-GENERALIZING

Question: Should our town adopt zoning?
Answer: "No! Because it didn't work in Oldtown and it won't work anywhere."

The generalization, though based on a single case, is applied to all towns everywhere, presumably for all time. In this particular case, investigation happened to show that the reasons for abandoning zoning in "Oldtown" were complicated, unique, and political. Often people add a value judgment to the fallacy of over-generalizing, and reason that what may be partly unsuccessful is *all* wrong, or *per contra*, what is good in spots is flawless throughout.

The proverb, "One swallow does not make a summer," is an excellent short reminder of this fallacy. I personally remember first my grandfather's story about "our old cat and another one," a company which grew to a million cats.

2. THIN ENTERING WEDGE

Question: Should our town adopt zoning?
Answer: "No! Because next thing you know they'll be telling us when we can blow our noses!"

This reply received hearty applause from the opposition at the town meeting where zoning was adopted. It follows the adage: "Give them an inch and they'll take an ell." To date hardly any small Connecticut towns have installed even a building code, though some have had the comparatively mild zoning regulation for a generation. The above extrapolation makes no sense, though it is an effective wisecrack.

A reminder of the fallacy might be: "If you give women the vote it will break up the home!" We did, and it didn't.

3. Getting Personal (Ad Hominem)

Question: Should we adopt zoning?

Answer: "*Look who's behind it; they say Joe Cook was indicted for bootlegging back in the thirties.*" This reply uses an unverified rumor from the omniscient "they," a rumor which, even if true, has nothing to do with the question in hand. If a supporter can be discredited, it is hoped that zoning itself will be discredited.

The classic example of *ad hominem,* found in all the textbooks, is the advice to the lawyer about to go to trial: "No case. Abuse the plaintiff's attorney."

4. You're Another (Tu Quoque)

Question: Shall we adopt zoning?

Answer: "*Mr. Moderator, we are criticized by some citizens of neighboring towns for being behind the times in not adopting zoning. I should like to ask, Mr. Moderator, why some of these same towns don't plow out their roads in winter.*"

In *tu quoque* one answers a charge by revolving it upon the questioner, thus dodging the issue. A famous example is the guide in the new Moscow subway answering the American tourist: "What about the trains?" "Well, what about the share-croppers in Alabama?"

5. Scrambling Cause and Effect (Post Hoc)

Question: Shall we adopt zoning?

Answer: "*Look at Northton. They put in zoning and the next thing you knew the town treasurer skipped to Canada with twenty-two thousand dollars.*"

The defaulting treasurer skipped after zoning went into effect, true enough, but there is no causal relationship, and the implication that he took a joy ride on zoning funds is ludicrous. In small towns with unpaid citizen members, zoning boards are economical if not always efficient. In our town the total cost has been about five hundred dollars a year.

Chantecler, the rooster in Rostand's play, was sure that his crow at dawn was responsible for the sunrise.

6. FALSE ANALOGY

Question: Should we adopt zoning?

Answer: "No! It's like a mirage in the desert. It looks wonderful at a distance, but when you get close up there's nothing there but trouble."

Analogies can often widen one's view of an issue, but they must have a reasonable connection. This analogy has none. In Chapter 10 we quoted the letter writer who compared a proposed chain of radar stations around the U.S. to the Great Wall of China. The Great Wall did not protect China, he said, therefore the radar chain will not protect America. Again no real connection.

7. APPEAL TO AUTHORITY (AD VERECUNDIAM)

Question: Should we adopt zoning?

Answer: "Why, the very idea would make old Israel Putnam turn in his grave. He believed in freedom!" (General Putnam is a local figure, as he had winter headquarters in our town during the American Revolution.)

Rather than discuss the modern problem, the speaker would let General Putnam, dead before the invention of the locomotive, decide it in the negative. Dead men, of course, cannot speak for themselves, and wise men can be wrong. We remember how Columbus rejected the Orinoco against the factual evidence, because Pliny had not mentioned it.

8. "FIGURES PROVE"

Question: Should we adopt zoning?

Answer: "No. The Whollop Poll shows that 74.86 percent of towns which adopted it wish they hadn't."

In this fictitious case, the two decimal places make a dubious argument look impressive. But who runs the poll and how responsible is he? When was the question asked? How large was the sample? How did the pollster define "wish"? Who precisely are "they"? Did he drop the *"don't knows"* down the drain?

We do not have to look far for our key illustration. Mark Twain "figured" that if the Mississippi River kept on shortening its course as in the recent past, by A.D. 2600 it would only be a mile and three quarters from Cairo, Illinois to New Orleans!

9. APPEAL TO THE CROWD (AD POPULUM)

Question: Should we adopt zoning?
Answer: "No! It's just a scheme of the rich to run all the little people out of town!"

To the barricades, comrades! But records in many towns over many years fail to indicate any "little people" driven out, though some new ones have doubtless been discouraged from entering. Acreage restrictions have sometimes prevented low-cost subdivisions from being built in certain parts of town. Two considerations are often neglected in discussing the issue; first, that zoning never interferes with the *status quo*, it applies only to future construction; second, that the experience of other towns, *if carefully studied*, can answer most of the objections raised.

A famous slogan to illustrate *ad populum* is Bryan's famous peroration: "You shall not crucify mankind upon a cross of gold!"

10. ARGUING IN CIRCLES (CIRCULUS IN PROBANDO)

Question: Should we adopt zoning?

Answer: *"Zoning may be all right for some towns, but not for other towns, and our town is one of the towns it isn't all right for."*

The argument has an authentic grass-roots ring, but it is swallowing its own tail. It says in effect, "Zoning is not good for our town because it isn't good for our town."

Arguing in circles usually boils down to: "It must be true because it says so itself." "Why is the Koran infallible?" "Because it was written by Allah's Prophet, Mahomet." "How do you know Mahomet was Allah's Prophet?" "Because the Koran says so."

11. "Self-evident Truths"

Question: Should we adopt zoning?
Answer: *"No! Everybody knows it's a lot of nonsense."*

The debater takes it for granted that the question is not worth an argument. "Everybody" has already decided it in the negative. He leans comfortably on a proposition which he believes, or hopes to convince others, is self-evident. A little factual investigation, however, would tell him that the majority of citizens in his state have freely voted in favor of the proposition, and about a hundred million Americans now live under zoning regulations of some kind.

I recall this fallacy by thinking of the course of the planets around the sun. The early astronomers considered it self-evident that their paths were perfect circles. But later calculations proved they travel in ellipses.

12. Black or White

Question: Should we adopt zoning?
Answer: *"No! Zoning is dictatorship. We live in a democracy and there's no middle ground. We have to choose and I choose democracy, Mr. Moderator!"*

This ringing declaration also received a big hand from the anti-zoners. The trouble with it is that zoning is not a black-or-white proposition. Our town already has many regulations; no human society indeed can exist without rules, prohibitions, taboos—written or unwritten. Will these proposed new regulations make living easier, or more difficult, for the majority of citizens? That is the real question, and it deals in tones of gray.

A good illustration which often comes to my mind is the tone of gray in the liberty-versus-regimentation argument: "Your liberty to swing your arms ends where my nose begins."

13. Guilt by Association

Question: Should our town adopt zoning?

Answer: "*No! Because every Communist is in favor of it. Do we want to be known as headquarters for the Reds?*"

This reply directly contradicts the reply to number 9, *ad populum,* which argued that zoning would drive out the "little people"—for whom the Comrades are supposed to battle. Never mind; contradictions do not mean much when fallacies are on the loose. A careful poll would probably show a solid majority of real Communists *against* zoning as a rotten capitalist invention. But this is beside the point too. If the debater can insert the idea into the discussion that pro-zoners are playing the Communist game, he is helping to defeat the measure.

The false syllogism about Senator Taft favoring public housing, developed at length in the preceding chapter, is an easy case to remember.

HAZY AT THE EDGES

Just to run over the thirteen logical lapses in the above thumbnail form, let alone discussing them at chapter length, is to realize again how readily they stray into one another's territory. Nearly all can be interpreted as over-generalizing to some degree, while the distinction between *ad populum* and self-evident truths is a pretty fine one. In my grouping, furthermore, "figures prove" is frankly a subdivision of *ad verecundiam*, and "thin entering wedge" a subdivision of over-generalizing.

If the meticulous student objects to the classification, I can sympathize with him. But it would perhaps be fair to ask him to make one of his own. The first thing he will find, as I found, is that the classical fallacies with the Latin names have certain inconsistencies and duplications.[2] The modern reader, especially if he has a little background of science and semantics, feels the need for a tighter list. Nor do the learned authorities always agree. For instance, some of them list a fallacy called *non sequitur* (it doesn't follow) as part of the begging-the-question group, while others make it a kind of portmanteau, embracing all the fallacies.

The above list has not been reached without considerable study, experiment, and consultation with my betters in the matter of technical logic. If the reader can devise a clearer one, I will be the first to welcome it. Meanwhile the thirteen, for all their hazy edges, are distinct enough to help us recognize many common distortions of the reasoning process, and steer our minds along a straighter and more consistent path.

I have undoubtedly used every one of the fallacies in my time, and may even have repeated several in developing them in this book.[3] Once alerted, however, I now find myself detecting them more and more readily. It is not unpleasant to catch someone committing a *circulus* or a *post hoc*—even when the someone is yourself.

[2] See Appendix.
[3] If the reader finds one, please let me know. It will be useful in any revision.

19

In the Courtroom

THERE are three chief places in democratic societies where logical fallacies are held at bay as a matter of principle: the courtroom, the copy desk, and the laboratory. The copy desk has a fine tradition—not invariably lived up to—of holding to facts in the news columns, and reserving opinions for the editorial page. The laboratory, as we have seen, must exclude fallacious reasoning if science is to progress. Any use of *ad hominems* and "self-evident truths" would mean to fudge experiments and nullify conclusions.

As for number one, the courtroom, we have already glanced in while court was in session, to listen briefly to the reasoning employed by the professional reasoners there. Now I will try to pull these scattered observations together with a layman's summary of the principles and logic found in the courtroom. There are in effect two separate sets of principles and logic: those of Anglo-Saxon law, developed over the centuries, and the methods of up-and-coming trial lawyers to get around the rules of evidence.

Most of us are not jailed very often, however decorated our car may be with parking tickets. So we have little first-hand knowledge of the magnificent safeguards which Anglo-Saxon law throws around an accused person. These safeguards were not always there. Some early chapters in English history record black injustices practiced in every rank of society including the highest. Kings and tyrants did not scruple to remove by assassination their political rivals, real or potential. The famous painting of the two little princes, imprisoned in the Tower of London, innocent victims of a power struggle for the throne, symbolizes those evil deeds.

Gradually the reforms appeared. First the nobles in 1215 wrung Magna Carta from King John, curbing his power. Then the revolution of the middle classes under Cromwell put further checks on tyrants and demagogues. Later, poor people were given equality before the law. American courts took over this legal apparatus, bag and baggage, and put part of it firmly in the Constitution.

The heart of Anglo-Saxon criminal law is the technique by which guilt is proved. By and large it follows the correct order of steps for straight thinking: first the relevant facts, then rigorous deductions from the facts, and finally conclusions and judgments. Much of what passes for "evidence" and "proof" on the street, in a public debate, or in committees of Congress, would go sailing out the window of even the lowliest police court. If counsel or witness begins his remarks with "Your Honor, everybody knows . . ." he will be stopped in his tracks. This is the fallacy of "self-evident truth," which no judge in his senses can tolerate. Nobody knows anything until the facts are put on the record.

Few of these historic safeguards have been used in the Congressional trials, and loyalty board hearings, of recent years. Congressional investigations, as preliminary to specific legislation, are of course an old, tested, and invaluable procedure. But legislative trial of persons accused of "subversive tendencies" is relatively new. Such trials and hearings are justified by their advocates as corrections to the delays and technicalities of the courts. They are indeed faster; but a price is paid, both by the accused and by society. Says Alan Barth:[1]

[1] *Government by Investigation.* Viking, 1955.

The legislative trial is a device for condemning men without the formalities of due process. It has become the accepted means of dealing with persons suspected of Communist affiliations or of that even vaguer offense, Communist sympathies. Courts of law are, in the view of zealots, slow, cumbersome, and uncertain instruments for this purpose. . . .

Various government loyalty and security boards have shown some quaint notions of what constitutes proof. A woman, for instance, was kept from her government job for months while the local Security Board investigated charges by her landlady.[2] The landlady had deposed that the woman was holding Communist meetings in her apartment. Asked how she knew they were Communist meetings, the landlady explained that it was obvious, because they used only one candle and kept their voices low.

ANGLO-SAXON JUSTICE

If you have ever been in a large law library you have seen some of the thousands of volumes devoted to jurisprudence. It is of course quite impossible to summarize centuries of legal evolution in a few paragraphs, and if I were a lawyer I am sure I would not dare attempt it. Yet it may not be too presumptuous to set down some of the outstanding principles which guide a trial in court today, principles broad enough and few enough to be readily remembered. They are not strictly "logic," except in the broad sense of a body of logic, a way to approach a person accused of crime.

1. When the accused is brought to trial, he is presumed to be innocent until competent evidence—not candles and low voices—proves him guilty "beyond a reasonable doubt." The courtroom parallels the laboratory in using high probabilities rather than absolutes.

[2] Adam Yarmolinsky: *Case Studies in Personnel Security* (Bureau of National Affairs, Washington, 1955).

2. The accused does not have to prove his own innocence; the prosecution must do the proving. "The general rule is that he who asserts a fact must prove it, and not he who denies."[3]

3. Evidence turns on acts committed, not on opinions, beliefs, philosophies, or loose talk. A witness is supposed to tell what he saw or heard, not what he believes. Expert witnesses, however, may express an opinion of what the facts indicate. In a murder trial involving death by a bullet, a properly qualified expert in ballistics is permitted to testify that from the markings on the bullet, and grooves in the barrel of the revolver, he is of the opinion that the fatal shot was fired from that particular gun. Similarly a qualified psychiatrist is permitted to testify whether in his opinion the accused was sane when the crime was committed.

4. In a criminal trial before a jury, the judge lays down the law involved, and guides the jury in finding the facts by allowing, or disallowing, the evidence which counsel seeks to present. Whether there is competent evidence is for the judge to say. Whether the facts as found demonstrate guilt or innocence is for the jury to decide.

5. The accused may cross-examine his accusers face to face; evidence against him on the basis of secret information is disallowed. If he cannot afford counsel, the Court will provide him with one.

6. The accused has the right of appeal to a higher court.

7. In examining witnesses, counsel is not allowed to ask leading questions, which suggest the answer counsel wishes to receive.

To these seven safeguards should be added those specified in the American Bill of Rights—freedom of speech, press, assembly, and religion; security from unreasonable search and

---

[3] *Encyclopedia Britannica* on "Evidence."

seizure; the right to a speedy and public trial by jury; freedom from "double jeopardy," or being tried twice for the same crime; freedom from testifying against oneself, and from excessive bail or fines, and from "cruel and unusual punishment."

BACK TO THE DARK AGES

Americans as we have seen are losing some of these freedoms. "McCarthyism," as defined in a preceding chapter, has attempted to set up a different kind of law in a different kind of court, to replace, if not reverse, the principles of Anglo-Saxon justice. Cases which would not be admitted in the regular courts have been brought under administrative jurisdiction, i.e., loyalty boards, or before investigating committees of Congress and state legislatures. Many an accused person has been declared guilty with no proof beyond the charge, and then tried for his associations, ideas, suspected intentions, family connections, rather than for his specific acts.

Senator Thomas C. Hennings of Missouri, after looking into the loyalty-security program of the federal government, in hearings before his subcommittee on Constitutional Rights, summed up his early findings in these words:

Free Americans have been brought to judgment by government officials without even the safeguards given accused criminals in our courts . . . The use of undisclosed witnesses in security hearings . . . the shifting of the burden of proof to the accused . . . the doctrines of guilt by association and by kinship . . . these are some of the aspects of the growing new body of law.[4]

Seen on television, the legislative trials looked judicial enough, at least they looked like a Hollywood version of a trial. Actually, however, they were a legal no-man's land, without tradition or rules. An accused person absolved by one committee might be promptly worked over by another

[4] AP dispatch, November 3, 1955

committee, or summoned back by the first committee on the flimsiest pretense of new "evidence"—and thus be denied any protection against double jeopardy. Responsible lawyers, trying to defend clients before these revolutionary tribunals, felt as though they were living in a nightmare, so alien was it to all their experience in court.

Critics declared it returned the law to the Dark Ages, and introduced into America the inquisitorial methods of totalitarian states today. We remember the answer of the Emperor Julian to Delfidius, the prosecutor, in a famous Roman law case: "Can anyone be proved innocent if it be enough to have accused him?" In spite of the excuse of catching a lot of spies and conspirators, actually the tribunals exposed almost none.

A collateral effect has often been to carry the accusation from the investigating committees into the press. In a few cases this has helped the accused person. Certain army officers, for instance, came out of the McCarthy hearings better than the Senator himself. David Lilienthal's classic statement, "This I Do Believe," was his defense against a critical senatorial investigator, and it made history. In other cases, publicity has virtually resulted in "trial by headline"—a type of mental torture which even the Inquisition, lacking press and radio, could not impose. Some radio commentators meanwhile have set up kangaroo courts on the air, with witnesses, quoted documents, "evidence," usually on the level of "one candle and low voices," all complete.

AD IGNORANTIAM

Both the formal logicians and Anglo-Saxon law reject a fallacy known as *argumentum ad ignorantiam*. It is something like *tu quoque* (you're another), in that the challenge is revolved on the challenger, thus:

"The State Department is full of Reds!"

"Prove it."

"I don't have to, let's see you disprove it."

And again:

"Allah selected Mahomet as his prophet."

"How do you know?"

"Well, you can't prove he didn't!"[5]

Instead of proving your argument, you challenge your opponent to disprove it. If he can't, then you triumphantly assert that you have won. You do no demonstrating at all— which I suppose is where the "ignorance" comes in. Nice work if you can get it, and strictly forbidden in court. It amounts to forcing the accused to prove his innocence. The new administrative tribunals, however, and the practice nicknamed "trial by headline," thrive on *ad ignorantiam*.

THE FALLACY OF "MULTIPLE QUESTIONS"

Though Anglo-Saxon law employs the principles of straight thinking described in this book, sharp attorneys are constantly trying to get around the rules, often by using one or another of the fallacies we have been at pains to analyze. Thus one of the five lawyers defending the men accused of murdering the Negro boy Emmett Till is reported to have addressed a Mississippi jury: "Your fathers will turn over in their graves if you return a verdict of guilty."[6] The judge must have been napping, for this is illegitimate *ad verecundiam*. To produce evidence of a corpse turning over in its grave would not be easy.

There is another classical fallacy much favored by fast-working trial lawyers if they can get away with it. It is part of the begging-the-question group and is usually called the

---

[5] Following Lionel Ruby.
[6] *New York Times*, September 25, 1955.

fallacy of "multiple questions." The trick is to combine two or more questions into one, and demand a yes-or-no answer. The outstanding example in all the textbooks is a familiar one:

"Have you stopped beating your wife? Answer yes or no!"

If you answer *yes*, you admit you used to beat her; if *no*, you admit you still beat her. To find the true facts demands *two* questions: (1) "Have you ever beaten your wife?" (2) "If so, have you stopped?" The prudent course for a witness confronted with a multiple question is to say: "What do you mean?" and get it broken down into component questions.

Another example: "When did you give up drinking?" If you set a date you are done for.

"What do you think of that crook Robinson?" is out of bounds, and so is: "You saw the defendant at the meeting looking pretty suspicious, didn't you?" And so is: "What time was it when you met this man?" when the intent is to bring out the admission that such a meeting had taken place.

In Congressional investigations of subversion the technique of the leading question has often been used. Here is an actual case. A witness denied that he was a Communist, and cited as evidence that he had been vigorously denounced by the Communist paper, the *Daily Worker*. Whereupon the chairman observed: "Let us put it this way: if I were an ardent member of the Communist party would I not have taken the same action?"

It is true, of course, that party members have been known to camouflage themselves by pretending to be anti-Communist. The witness knew this and he was under oath. Thus he could not answer "no" to the Chairman's question, but if he answered "yes" he would be trapped by this fallacious syllogism:

Communists cover up by spurious anti-Communist activities.
The witness has engaged in anti-Communist activities.
Therefore the witness is a Communist.

The art of cross-examination can become a systematic exploitation of the fallacy of multiple or leading questions, as counsel seeks to force an opposing witness to aid counsel's case. In the courtroom there is a judge to halt such exploitation, but in the legislative trials and security hearings, the sky is usually the limit.

Meanwhile out on the hustings, smart politicians are not strangers to the fallacy of multiple questions:

"Are you for the Republicans and Peace and Prosperity?"

"Are you for the Democrats and the Bill of Rights?"

As I write, the courts are moving to the defense and rehabilitation of loyal citizens scarred by extra-legal procedures and abuses of power. Judgment in case after case is being reversed. It is a heartening spectacle, and if I may be permitted a legitimate *ad verecundiam*, it shows again the wisdom of our forefathers in giving Americans the protection of Anglo-Saxon law. If there is to be any turning over in graves it should be when this great legacy is denied. The law may sometimes seem tardy, but it is still there, firm ground beneath our feet.

20
Masters of Propaganda

A JOURNALIST friend of mine was accosted by a local
official at a cocktail party in East Germany after the war. This
functionary, glass in hand, angrily denounced the United States
for lynching a Negro. My friend, who had heard no such
news, could say little in his embarrassment. At this point a
Russian in colonel's uniform intervened, pushed the German
aside, and said: "Pay no attention to him; he doesn't know
what he is talking about. My office in Moscow manufactured
that story." Experts in propaganda usually take a news story
and slant it, but the great masters make it up out of whole
cloth.

To a student of semantics, there is no such *thing*—note
the italics—as "propaganda." It is a word in our heads, corresponding to no entity in the outside world, a word to which
everyone probably gives a somewhat different meaning. It
can, however, be a useful label to designate special kinds of
behavior. The label is at least three centuries old. Cardinals of
the Catholic Church in charge of foreign missions were officially
known as the College of Propaganda, an organization founded
in 1622 and concerned with good works.

In America today, however, the word has acquired overtones of evil.[1] Elmo Roper once ran a controlled experiment.
He matched two groups of respondents with approximately

---

[1] "Propaganda . . . now often used in a derogatory sense, connoting decep-
tion or distortion." Webster's *New World Dictionary*, 1953.

similiar opinions and, speaking of the Voice of America, asked group A: "Some people say it is better to explain the U.S. point of view as well as give the news: do you agree?" Forty-three percent answered *yes*. For group B he changed the wording a little: "Some people say it is better to include some propaganda as well as give the news: do you agree?" The *yeses* fell to 25 percent.

When somebody exerts pressure through the mass media to get you to do something for him or for his cause; when he flashes signals, sends up smoke screens, employs the thirteen fallacies with additional trimmings, to change your beliefs or behavior—you are being subjected to propaganda as here defined. He wants to shift your attitude, your vote, your bank account, in a direction favorable to him and unfavorable to his opponents. Sometimes what he says is true, but it is never disinterested truth. The attentive listener can usually hear in the background the grinding of an ax.

In developing the logical fallacies earlier, I have been concerned chiefly with issues not yet decided. I have warned, in making up our minds about them, to beware of mental mantraps. In propaganda the issue has already been decided by the propagandist; his inquiry is over. *This is it,* and his goal is to make you agree that this is it. Sometimes he calls on you to agree at the level of facts, more often at the level of inference or value judgments. The strongest pressure of all comes when action is desired; here indeed, words are weapons.

Though some people apparently like to be fooled, most of us prefer to take a hard look at the hand which pulls the strings. In this chapter I will describe some varieties of behavior covered by the label "propaganda," and in the next will try to analyze the techniques. If the reader can see what makes the puppets dance, he may be better prepared to defend himself.

THE MOSCOW MILL

Moscow runs a large and successful propaganda mill. It far exceeds the apparatus of Dr. Goebbels, which in its time exceeded anything the world had previously seen. The Moscow mill is operated by a huge bureaucracy, trained in some six thousand special schools.[2] In 1950 the Russian Government spent almost a billion dollars on propaganda, internal and external, and the satellite countries spent half a billion more. This does not include Communist organizations in Western nations. France and Italy have huge Red parties, spending large sums to rally the faithful and make converts.

The major goal of Moscow's propaganda, like that of any government, is to consolidate and extend its own power. The old ideal of socialist internationalism has been distorted into a fifth column technique. The propaganda machine faces two ways: *inward* to influence the Russian people, *outward* to influence the rest of the world. Five outward drives can be identified:

1. To stir up revolutions in other countries—say Guatemala.

2. To break up coalitions against Russia by encouraging quarrels between allies. As I write Moscow is trying to drive a wedge between the Middle East and the free nations.

3. To weaken Western nations by setting group against group—Moslems against Hindus, Catholics against Protestants, Negroes against whites, Arabs against Jews.

4. To picture the Soviet Union as an invincible power, armed with invincible weapons and an invincible idea. Russia, according to the propaganda, made all the great inventions, from the wheel to the turbo-jet engine.

---

[2] U.S. Advisory Commission on Information, Mark A. May, Chairman, *Report.* House Document No. 94, 83rd Congress.

5. To convince the world that Russia is the fountainhead of peace.

The "new look" in Moscow, following the death and degrading of Stalin, with friendship and cocktails for all, seems to be a kind of icing over the old propaganda pudding. The two lines are being carried on simultaneously. If the new line should some day win out, and the good will become genuine, then the subject of my next few pages would have chiefly historical interest. I would welcome the correction, but I do not expect it.

ARCH-ENEMY

The British authority, Edward Crankshaw, says that after World War II Moscow had planned to make Britain the arch-enemy, hoping that the U.S. would retreat to a policy of isolation as it did in 1919. President Truman's vigorous action to save Greece, followed by the Marshall Plan, shifted the propaganda target to America. The U.S. has been in the zone of heavy verbal fire since 1946. Crankshaw explains:

> In Kremlin circles an arch-enemy is a very precious thing, to be built up and cherished. It is the scapegoat to be blamed for all the ills of the world, including the harsh consequences of the Kremlin's own domestic policy. The line in such matters, too, is always that what now is, must always have been. Thus it is not enough to call President Truman a cannibal; it has to be proved that cannibalism is a long-time American tradition . . .[3]

"HATE-AMERICA" CAMPAIGN

In January, 1951, a special "Hate-America" campaign was launched by the Kremlin. In its stocks of ammunition we can recognize the fallacy *ad verecundiam*. They contained piles of doctored documents and photographs, dubious historical

[3] *New York Times* Magazine, August 17, 1952.

records, "eyewitness accounts," and phony statistics. Thirteen books appeared about the unspeakable Yankee, including novels and plays, in addition to new textbooks for school children. These contradicted the wartime texts in which Americans were friends, sending food and supplies. Besides the standard vilification, three new charges were introduced: (1) the U.S. cheated Russia out of Alaska; (2) American troops at Archangel in 1919 buried Russian civilians alive; (3) posters advertising Coca-Cola in the United States show Christ on the cross, asking for a drink.[4]

The last accusation is interesting for several reasons. An inscription in the Red Square reads: RELIGION IS THE OPIUM OF THE PEOPLE, but propaganda for foreign consumption does not hesitate to accuse American advertisers of sacrilege—thus working both sides of the street. The story derived, I am sure, from a British story I heard first in 1928, making fun of American advertising—only that one mentioned Snyder's Vinegar, not Coca-Cola. Thus, after twenty years, an old chestnut is revived as "evidence."

Moscow also had a field day with Governor Thomas E. Dewey. During the 1948 presidential campaign he was photographed with a group of Oregon businessmen, dressed in animal skins and waving bones. These characters call themselves "The Cavemen," and hope to attract visitors to the local caves. The photograph, said the master minds of the Kremlin, shows the savage and barbaric character of America, where a presidential candidate could join a society devoted to drinking blood and gnawing bones!

Such propaganda may sound crazy to us, but it was of course not beamed at us. It was beamed at simple citizens around the world who know very little about America, beyond the violent and distorted movies which Hollywood exports. All

[4] From the Mark May report.

unknowingly, Hollywood has softened up the customers for a brisk working over by Moscow. A U.S. information officer in Europe once suggested ironically that Washington negotiate a treaty with Hollywood to lessen the damage done by its films abroad.

The Kremlin has long insisted that Wall Street rules the U.S.; that the National Association of Manufacturers, along with millionaires, monopolists, and profiteers, constitute America's "ruling circles." "Peace-loving" peoples co-operate with the Kremlin; "warmongers" and "aggressors" do not. Co-operating governments are "peoples democracies," non-co-operators are "fascist states," or "capitalist imperialists."

"Democracy," in the Kremlin lexicon, means a job for all citizens who toe the line. Political democracy, with free voting and free speech as practiced by the West, has been branded a hypocritical scheme for insuring capitalistic control. Western leaders are called such names as "lackeys of imperialism," and "stooges of a moribund, decadent, crisis-ridden capitalist society."

Under the "new look," the attack is likely to continue. An academy for the study of "contemporary capitalism," reports C. L. Sulzberger, has been opened in Moscow, and is industriously devising a weird caricature of America.[5] How does a Russian leader who has never crossed the Atlantic, inquires Sulzberger, "get the idea that Averell Harriman wants to control the economy of Hungary, or that Estes Kefauver favors new formulas to consolidate 'colonial domination'?"

According to the Soviet magazine, *International Affairs*, "it has been almost enough to send a man to the electric chair to speak seriously of peace" in the United States. Meanwhile heads of AF of L-CIO, "separated by many years of bureaucratic leadership from the workers, collaborate with the most

[5] Dispatch from Moscow to the *New York Times*, January 2, 1956.

reactionary elements of government like Attorney General Brownell, and FBI Director Hoover." Brownell, it appears, does "everything in his power to wreck any labor union that fails to follow his political beliefs."

Sulzberger then quotes this curious Russian example of American customs: "Parents who want to determine what sort of a career their child is likely to follow place a dollar bill and a bottle of whisky before it. If the child picks up the dollar, that is a good sign—it will grow up to be a hard-working and prosperous citizen. If it reaches for the bottle, it will most likely grow up a confirmed drunkard.

"There is admiration here in Moscow," says Sulzberger, "for the power of the United States, respect for our technical ability, and envy of our living standards. But the contempt and misunderstanding of our politics, economics, social system and ideology—as expressed in party literature—is beyond belief."

Undoubtedly there are plenty of observers in Moscow well informed about the U.S. The propaganda picture is for local Russian consumption, and for ignorant, insecure, and unhappy people around the world. The first rule of Moscow is that anything connected with "capitalism" is evil, by definition, and therefore any propaganda which hurts capitalistic countries is perfectly legitimate.

INSIDE UTOPIA

"In Russia," says ex-Senator William Benton after a visit, "the rulers seek to convert the total culture into a giant propaganda apparatus."[6] The Minister of Culture runs the movies, the theatre, music, radio, TV, books and publishing, painting and graphic arts. The Party runs the policies of all the newspapers. "Every column, every story, every editorial will continue

---

[6] Article for the *Encyclopedia Britannica*, 1956.

to promote the Party line, to the complete exclusion of anything that interferes with that line."

Meanwhile in the U.S.S.R. "the political indoctrination of
radio and TV becomes the 'commercial.' " The net effect of this
attempt to control the thoughts and behavior of two hundred
million people we will reserve for the next chapter. Some of
the propaganda takes, and some apparently does not.

CAESAR, HITLER, AND PERÓN

If Julius Caesar had had television to aid him he might never
have been overthrown. Modern dictators would be relatively
helpless without such technological inventions as Klieg lights,
high-speed presses, radio, movies, TV. Both Mussolini and
Hitler were masters at putting on a show, while the Red
Square is famous for spectacles far beyond the scope of Hollywood.

Hitler especially knew the psychological value of suspense.
He would assemble mammoth audiences at Munich or Ham-
burg and keep them on the edge of their chairs, waiting,
waiting, until the supreme moment when the lights flared on,
the music of twenty bands blared out, ten thousand storm
troopers came rigidly to attention, swastikas fluttered under
electric fans, and der Fuehrer in his simple uniform—always
simple in dramatic contrast to the surrounding magnificence—
came striding down an arrow of light, his hand at the Nazi
salute. It took a stout heart to stand up against this massed
attack on eye, ear, and central nervous system.

The dictatorship in Argentina began preparing, months before Eva Perón died, to make her death and funeral a political
weapon to bolster the regime.[7] She was dying as "the martyr
for the workers." The propaganda was gradually intensified.
Presently union locals and Perónista party branches began

[7] R. J. Alexander in the *New Leader*, September 8, 1952.

calling for special masses to pray for her life, and pressure was put on priests to co-operate. A skilled embalmer waited for days in a hotel room, to be rushed to the death chamber. Nine hours later her body was ready for the stupendous obsequies.

Street lights were draped in black; mourning portraits, printed in advance by the thousand, at once appeared on walls and billboards. A two-day work stoppage was decreed throughout the country. Broadcasting stations played funeral music, interrupted only by solemn readings from Evita's book, *The Purpose of My Life.* "With the stage set so diligently," says Alexander, "it was not difficult to evoke a demonstration of mass hysteria unknown in the history of the continent." At the funeral, many persons were reported crushed to death.

"CAMPAIGN ORATORY"

An American presidential campaign is of course a classic exhibit in political propaganda. To be sure it is less lethal than the shows put on by the dictators. Few voters lose their lives, and the election itself illustrates a certain standard of sportsmanship: the defeated candidate is expected to send a telegram of congratulation to the winner. The dictators have no monopoly on doubletalk, but in the democracies the talk is often discounted. Here politics is generally regarded as a game, while in the dictatorships it is war without quarter.

Our presidential conventions follow a standard pattern. The spread-eagle speeches, the parades up the aisles, the banners, the singsong of balloting, the carefully clocked demonstrations —all fuse into a formal ballet, with the actors as well drilled as automatons. An anthropologist might fairly compare it to a Polynesian tribal dance.

As for the language involved, Frank Sullivan in *The New Yorker* puts his cliché expert, Mr. Arbuthnot, on the trail:

How does your candidate stand, Mr. Arbuthnot? *On his own two feet!*

Can he grasp a nettle? *Fearlessly. He faces facts. He will lead us out of the morass. His deeds are writ large!*

Where? *In the hearts of his countrymen!*

The opposition candidates, Mr. Arbuthnot finds, are "selfish opportunists, trampling on our God-given liberties" . . . When not trampling they are "whittling away." . . . "They stifle initiative. They suffer Agencies (Key) to be infiltrated by travelers (fellow), who follow philosophies (alien), and ideologies (false) . . . They undermine the foundations . . . only eternal vigilance . . ." After an evening with Mr. Arbuthnot almost anybody could write a campaign speech for either side.

SLOGANS IN 1952

Let us look at the record of a sample campaign—that of 1952. Republican propaganda in that year gave sinister implications to such slogans as: The Mess in Washington, New Dealism, Creeping Socialism, the Welfare State, Handouts-to-Foreigners, the Crushing Burden of Debt, and Me-Too-ism. The last was vigorously used in the campaign, but it had a boomerang. Anyone who said a kind word for social security, or any other popular legislative act of the last twenty years, could be tagged with Me-Too-ism, and so judged little better than a Communist. This identification continued to plague the Eisenhower administration when it came into office.

Democratic party oratory in 1952 was not quite so vivid. Being in office, orators were on the defensive and had to refer now and then to a few facts—the natural enemies of propaganda. Democratic orators did their best, however, to build an idyllic picture of life in America under their party: "You never had it so good." Their predictions of what would happen, if the Republicans should come to power, were as gruesome as the historical summaries of Republican orators about what *had* happened while the Democrats were in power. Big Business and the Interests were given a thorough going over; the Taft-Hartley Law was usually called the "slave labor law"; while criticisms of the protective tariff were taken out of mothballs and given a vigorous airing, reminiscent of the days of William Jennings Bryan.

REAL ISSUES VS. PHONY

These slogans, both Republican and Democratic, were blown up till they resembled the swaying monsters in Macy's Thanksgiving parade in New York City. Like Macy's monsters, too, they were filled with gas. Only candidate Stevenson made an attempt to "talk sense," and actually did so a good deal of the time. He tried to replace propaganda with information, reflection, and honest doubt. This was unique in all my long observation of the American political scene. The point is not whether Stevenson was right, but that, in the middle of a political campaign, he tried to gather facts, use logic upon them, and consider the issue under discussion in a grown-up way. Time and again he said he did not know the answer. Citizens accustomed to candidates who knew all the answers were stunned by the admission.

In the main, the real questions before America in the fall of 1952 were either ignored, or distorted in the hope of wringing votes out of them. Such looming issues as atomic energy and the H-bomb, proposals to break the deadlock of the cold war, the pressure of population on the food supply around the world, Japan's economic future, steps to halt a depression if the arms race should slacken, an intelligent program for agriculture, the definition of "loyalty" and "security," the crisis in the public schools—were almost never honestly examined, if they were mentioned at all.

Do citizens prefer the swaying verbal monsters, as professional politicians firmly believe? It would take an expensive project in public opinion research to find out, but here is an interesting sidelight. A fundamental rule of the professionals is that citizens demand, and deserve, lower taxes. Yet Elmo Roper in 1953 found a substantial majority of Americans *against* lower taxes at the expense of adequate defense. Perhaps the sovereign voter is not so bemused by logical fallacies as the politicians believe. Perhaps if not an orator had opened his ample mouth from June to November of 1952, General Eisenhower would have been elected by the same comfortable margin.

THE PAIN AND BEAUTY BOYS

Campaign oratory in the democracies is less sinister than the propaganda mills of Moscow, and it might be argued that advertising is less damaging to a given society than campaign oratory with its neglect of real issues. But advertising uses many of the same methods of argument, often in ways that are easier to observe. It also has a useful function in telling us about new products. Most of the words and pictures, however, which fill the newspapers, magazines, and air waves attempt to shift the consumer's dollar from product A to product B and back to A again, or stimulate him to buy something he doesn't really need. All the thirteen fallacies come into play, together with extra psychological snares, such as the new and much touted "motivational research."

Publicity campaigns for worthy causes—and some not so worthy—and for building up individuals, often skirt the edges of the truth with equal agility. Imitating advertisers, the idea is to "sell the package" without too much attention to what's inside it. In *The Golden Kazoo*, for instance, a novel by John

Schneider, we find a hilarious account of how Madison Avenue took over the presidential election of 1960, and sold both Republican and Democratic nominees—dull fellows they were—like so much toothpaste. "The first immutable law of advertising," says one of the characters, "is that *There aint any high-brow in low-brows, but there's some low-brow in everybody.*"

The worst offenders in advertising have been nicknamed in the trade "the pain and beauty boys," and here is a sample of each.

PERFUME ADVERTISING

. . . I think only of that moment—the moment when "the world forgetting, by the world forgot," we shall soar together to the stars. Until that moment comes, may your dreams reveal the message that surges from my very being. Yours alone, *Cobra.*

A reporter named Joseph Field, overwhelmed by this surging prose, went around to see the agency man in New York who wrote it. He was given a frank and engaging account of how perfume ads are dreamed up. "Writing perfume copy," said the agency man, "is much more entertaining than writing any other kind. Most perfume businessmen understand that promoting their product involves a certain amount of fantasy. As far as meaning goes, the first fundamental in perfume copy is that it doesn't have to mean anything . . . you are not governed by the laws of common sense.

"What we try to do," he continued, "is to get a woman to go to a store and ask for our brand. We try to amuse and startle her in the copy. Above all, almost all perfume copy contains an implied promise that using the particular brand will heighten her sex appeal. . . . Sometimes," he said, "we like to see how far we can go. That *Cobra* ad did create several violent reactions."

The copy writer was wrong on one important point: his perfume ad was alive with meaning, and it was also a prime example of *post hoc*, viz:

Successfully seductive ladies in the ads use *Cobra*.
I'll use *Cobra*.
Therefore I'll be successfully seductive.

And off she goes to the nearest drugstore.

MIRACLE TOOTHPASTE

So much for beauty and allure; how about pain? Our sample is typical. "Triumph Over Tooth Decay!" reads a full-page ad in January, 1956. "At last scientists have found the answer," with a picture of two "scientists" in white coats, flanked by a microscope, and holding up test tubes—a splendid sample of *ad verecundiam*.

The month before, however, the president of the New York State Dental Society had paid his respects to *all* toothpaste advertising, as follows:[8]

The last five years have seen a succession of so-called "magic ingredients" introduced to the public through shrieking headlines and alluring text in printed and televised commercials. These dentifrices have had one thing in common—their disappointing performance. Throughout the country our colleagues report bitter complaints from disillusioned patients who have acquired numerous new cavities, and other mouth diseases, despite regular use of the "miracle dentifrices" . . . Such false claims are almost criminally deceptive and misleading.

The Golden Kazoo supports the doctor. "Maybe you don't remember," says one high-powered ad-man to a colleague, "how you zigged and zagged from amazing ammoniated to

[8] New York *Herald Tribune*, December 8, 1955.

colossal chlorophyll to astonishing anti-enzyme to fantastic fluoridized to Formula 9 Perma-white. . . ."

Miracle Toothpaste and Miracle Candidates are subject to similar laws of high-pressure merchandising. Let us look more closely at these laws.

21

Anatomy of Propaganda

Social scientists have only recently attempted to take the propaganda machine apart and find out what makes it tick. Clyde Miller and Leonard Doob among others have made progress in this direction. Your author some years ago, in *Your Money's Worth*, collaborated with F. J. Schlink to analyze methods by which the advertiser overpowered the unwary consumer.

The great political propagandists of our time—Hitler, Goebbels, Stalin, Mussolini, Perón, McCarthy—have played mostly by ear. Hitler indeed boasted of his "intuition." In the Army-McCarthy hearings on TV, the junior Senator from Wisconsin could be seen catching out of thin air an idea no bigger than a man's hand—an idea which he would then develop extemporaneously into a massive thunderhead.

In this intuitive performance, as well as in a more scientific approach, various principles and techniques can be identified. Nevertheless, much needs to be done before propaganda is as well understood as, say, juvenile delinquency. The methods now to be listed are drawn from many examples of high-pressure mass persuasion, such as those described in the preceding chapter. It may be argued that such analysis can help an aspiring demagogue pinpoint his attack. It can; and so can the laws of mechanics help an aspiring safe-cracker. It could be argued that I should never have written *Your Money's Worth*, because of possible tips to unscrupulous advertisers. It is hoped that more readers will find suggestions here to protect themselves from propaganda than aspiring propagandists will find to further their art.

Experts at the controls of a propaganda campaign, such as the master minds in Moscow, may use any of the thirteen fallacies which suit their book, as well as the *leading-question* technique, described in the Courtroom chapter. In addition they are often well versed in some special procedures which we have not yet examined:

1. The deliberate use of unscrupulous means to further their ends.
2. The Big Lie.
3. The Scapegoat and Hero technique.
4. The creation of Martyrs.
5. The constant possession of the offensive.
6. Non-verbal symbols, such as the swastika.
7. "It's a plot!"—as an answer to criticism.
8. Doubletalk.

Of the fallacies earlier described, propagandists especially favor:

1. Guilt by association and by accusation.
2. Either-or thinking. This is practically mandatory: "those who are not with us are against us."
3. Appeal to authority, often through doctored "evidence" and tearing statements out of context. A famous case was the widely published photograph which showed Senator Tydings of Maryland in close conversation with Communist Earl Browder, doctored by political opponents to defeat Tydings in an election.
4. *Post hoc* reasoning. A notorious example, still nourished by the Democratic high command, is this false syllogism:

Herbert Hoover was elected President in 1928.
The U.S. suffered a terrible depression in 1929.
Therefore Hoover was the cause of the depression.

Which is an outrageous perversion of the facts.

The propaganda message usually aims to arouse emotion. Any
appeal to reason will be well subordinated, and carefully keyed
to strengthen the hearer's prejudices. The emotions most frequently played upon are:

Fear of out-groups—*we will save you from them!*

Feelings of insecurity—*we will make you safe!*

Feelings of inferiority—*we will put you on top!*

Most of us suffer from various frustrations which often
result in aggressive impulses of various intensities. If the
propagandist can open a channel for some mass frustration,
he can ride high on its torrential sweep. The classic example
is the way Hitler rode to power on the mass frustrations of the
German people. He had an ideal target for his propaganda in
the insecurity feelings of most Germans, following defeat in
war, the harsh terms of the Treaty of Versailles, and a runaway
inflation.

Some of the principles and techniques now to be discussed
can be found in most propaganda drives today. Earlier operators used them too, but they lacked the mass media. A Roman
Senator was heard in the Senate; an American Senator can be
heard around the world at approximately the speed of light.

MEANS VERSUS ENDS

Unscrupulous means are rarely employed in ordinary discussions. There the end is not known, it is something to come
out of the discussion. The typical propagandist has determined
his ends before the campaign begins—which is one good defini-

tion of propaganda, and he is trying to influence action—which is another.

Lenin is said to have declared: "It is necessary . . . to use any ruse, cunning, unlawful method, evasion, concealment of truth." Hitler was even more explicit: "On a given signal, bombard him with a regular drum-fire of calumnies. Keep it up until his nerves give way."

Powerful means are essential when the party line is changed. What was denounced as black yesterday must be lauded as white today. Members of the American Communist party have had to stifle their built-in American habits in order to follow the right-about-faces of the Moscow line. No calumny, for instance, was too violent to heap upon the Nazis up to 1939, and then, like a bolt from the blue, the Molotov-Ribbentrop Pact made the Nazis dear comrades in arms. As I write, the dethronement of Stalin is taking place, to the consternation of Communists all over the world.

According to diplomatic dispatches . . . on January 18, 1956, *Kommunist*, the Communist theoretical organ, was sent to press with an article praising Stalin. About January 25, a conference of Soviet historians met to consider the problems of rewriting the history of the Stalinist era, along the lines of the anti-Stalinist attacks delivered at the party Congress the following month [February 1956].[1]

In the West, historians meet to compare sources and get closer to the truth about the past. In Moscow they meet to reconstruct the past. Well, it keeps the printers busy, anyway.

American political battles developed over the years are rough, but they have their rules. You may call your opponent a rascal, a whittler-away of liberties, a tax-eater and exploiter, even a liar—but you must not call him a traitor. This rule was recently violated by the slogan "twenty years of treason,"

---

[1] Dana A. Schmidt in *New York Times*, March 21, 1956.

which carried us a long step toward the total propaganda standards of the dictators.

THE BIG LIE

A lie is a false statement made deliberately, but a Big Lie, as Hitler described it at length in *Mein Kampf,* is a work of art. The bigger and more improbable it is, he said, the more stunning the effect. The effect cannot be achieved, however, without pounding reiteration in the mass media. Among Hitler's masterpieces was the identification of the Germans with the "Aryan Race," glorified as superior to all other races. Moscow has a well-stocked storehouse of Big Lies, including:

The people of the U.S are starving.

The South Koreans crossed the 38th Parallel and invaded North Korea, bringing on the war.

American fliers practiced germ warfare in Korea.

Russians made all the great inventions.

In December, 1955, Soviet leaders accused the West of having started World War II by grooming Hitler as their "bloodhound." "Even the boldest lie," says the *New York Times* editorially, "cannot change history.[2] That war was sparked by the infamous Molotov-Ribbentrop Pact, in which the two most aggressive powers of the time arranged for the division of the spoils of the war they were preparing. What is more, this pact involved a monstrous Soviet double-cross of the Western powers, then seeking to stop Hitler and to avert a war."

Senator McCarthy on the home front proved himself an expert in the Big Lie technique. He might start it with a simple piece of paper. "I hold here in my hand a list of 205 persons who are known to the Secretary of State as being members of the Communist Party, and who nevertheless are still working

[2] December 8, 1955.

and shaping the policy of the State Department."[3] Asked to name the 205 persons, McCarthy reduced the number to 57; later advanced it to 81. *No member of the Communist party has ever been found in the State Department to correspond to the charge.* "Security risks" have been reported, but not one authentic Communist. Richard Rovere described a development of this technique, and called it the "multiple untruth." It consisted in a kind of rotating, retreating advance. As one charge is disproved, you substitute another, and so on until your confused audience has forgotten the first. Six or seven are usually enough and then you begin over again.

SCAPEGOAT AND HERO

This propaganda technique is ancient, as the name implies. On the Day of Atonement the Israelites chose a live goat by lot.[4] The high priest in his robes laid both hands on the goat's head and confessed the sins of the people, accumulated during the past year. The goat, full of transplanted sin, was then banished to the wilderness, and the people, much relieved, could go about their business. Said Allport:

Everywhere we see our human tendency to revert to this primitive level of thinking and to seek a scapegoat—some object or animal, or more often some luckless human being—who may be saddled with blame for our own misfortunes and misdeeds . . . Though a universal phenomenon, it is especially during times of stress— of war, famine, revolution, depression—that . . . scapegoating increases.

Russia has been in chronic crisis since 1914, enduring successively war, revolution, famine, purges, and again war. Italy and Germany were in crisis after World War I. The United States is in a crisis today, but a curious one. While economic

[3] Speech at Wheeling, West Virginia, February 9, 1950. As reported in the *Saturday Evening Post*, August 19, 1950.
[4] Following Gordon W. Allport, *The Nature of Prejudice* (Addison-Wesley and Beacon Press, 1954).

prosperity is great, world leadership has suddenly been thrust upon us, making citizens confused, uneasy, and alarmed. The Korean War particularly upset us.

The scapegoat of Stalin was the "capitalist class." The scapegoat of Hitler was "the Jews"; of Mussolini "the Communists." The scapegoat of Senator McCarthy was the *Communist within,* including everyone, as we have seen, who could be implicated through a very broad application of guilt by association.

Propaganda identifies the scapegoat, and simultaneously identifies the Hero who will save the people from impending doom. Throughout the Army-McCarthy Hearings in 1954 the Senator from Wisconsin seized every opportunity to remind the TV audience (estimated at twenty-six million), that it was he, McCarthy, who stood alone against the Communist conspiracy—"reaching for the nation's jugular vein."

THE CREATION OF MARTYRS

McCarthy doubled as Hero and Martyr. The Peronistas in Argentina made a martyr out of Evita, declaring that she gave up her life for the cause of labor. Communists, Nazis, even Chicago gunmen, stage stupendous funerals for their fallen heroes. A case of real or supposed injustice may be seized upon and inflated by publicity to the skies. We recall the "Scottsboro Boys," and the Rosenbergs. A martyrdom focuses popular attention on a specific, personal outrage, and is often more effective than tons of printed arguments.[5] "Remember the *Maine,*" in 1898, may have been responsible for a war.

HOLD THE OFFENSIVE

Always the attack! as the French General Staff used to say. The smart propagandist, repulsed on one position, has a new

[5] Don Mankiewicz analyzed this method at length in his novel, *Trial.*

offensive in readiness. When forced to get rid of J. B. Matthews, McCarthy launched an all-out assault on Allen Dulles and the Central Information Agency as a hotbed of subversion. Moscow too is quick at covering a retreat on one front with a brisk offensive on another. The "arch-enemy" abroad is always good for another pounding when things are not going so well at home. No big-time propagandist can afford to be wrong, or to give an inch.

NON-VERBAL SYMBOLS

Skilled propagandists associate their message with popular symbols, such as the hearthstone and the flag, or at times adopt new symbols—the hammer and sickle of the Communist, the swastika of the Nazis, special salutes, songs, and uniforms. Moscow converted both Lenin and Stalin into ikons or semi-deities. I once saw Lenin, very lifelike, embalmed in his shrine outside the Kremlin wall. A long line of weary people in smocks and shawls were patiently waiting to see him too. The staring portraits of Stalin, executed, as Mark Twain would say, by gifted sign painters, furnished new ikons for peasant huts throughout Russia. They are now coming down in a hurry. Who will be the next ikon?

It is interesting to note how a well-oiled propaganda machine, like that of Moscow, or of Goebbels, develops an apparatus almost theological. There is a supernatural hierarchy of gods and devils, together with sacred writings—*Mein Kampf, Das Kapital,* Evita Perón's *The Purpose of My Life.*

"IT'S A PLOT"

If a propagandist finds the opposition too rough to ride over, he may declare a conspiracy. Thus the attorney general of Georgia, fighting desegregation in the schools, accused the NAACP of plotting to force the Supreme Court to rule in favor of segregation. Congressman Carroll Reece of Tennessee sees

American charitable foundations as engaged in a ten-billion-dollar conspiracy to subvert the American way of life. "Interlocking directorates of Wall Street" used to be a powerful slogan in left-wing propagandist literature, with a spiderweb chart to back it up. McCarthy supporters have prepared similar spiderweb charts of internal subversives, from the wives of ex-Presidents down.

Mr. Zed, as a lone alleged subversive, is not nearly so newsworthy as Mr. Zed, a key figure in a secret organization boring its sinister way through key government bureaus. This is not to say that conspiracies never exist, only that they make fine copy for the propagandist, whether they exist or not.

When John Foster Dulles, Secretary of State, was interviewed in February, 1956, by a reporter from *Life* magazine, the reverberations shook the world. Mr. Dulles was reported to have said in effect that the art of keeping the peace is to have the courage to advance to the brink of war.

Mr. Butler, of the Democratic National Committee, sees in it a deep-laid Republican plot, but Mr. Butler would, of course. It is his official business to discover everywhere Republican plots full of moral turpitude and intellectual depravity, and he attends to his business assiduously; but it is doubtful that even he, as a person, not an official, puts much stock in the plot theory.[6]

DOUBLETALK

Classicists list a logical fallacy called *equivocation*, in which a single word, or term, is used in two senses in the same context.

All fair things are honorable.
This woman is fair.
Therefore she is honorable.

Here the word "fair" is used to mean (1) right and reasonable, and (2) a beautiful blonde.

[6] Gerald Johnson in the *New Republic*, February 6, 1956.

Anatole Rapoport gives another example:

Nothing is more important than life.
Holes in doughnuts are nothing.
Therefore holes in doughnuts are more important than life.

The meaning of "nothing," he points out, has changed in mid-syllogism. The word remains the same, while its meaning shifts like a mainsail coming about in the wind.

The oracle at Delphi encouraged Croesus to attack Cyrus, with the promise that if he crossed the Halys Peninsula he would "destroy a mighty empire."[7] The promise was a perfectly safe one, but unfortunately it was Croesus' own empire which fell. Oracles, soothsayers, and writers of Wall Street market letters must be well versed in doubletalk.

Propagandists in the U.S. are now engaged in a spirited drive to pass anti-labor legislation in the states, under the banner of the "right to work" law. Who can possibly be against the right to work? Meanwhile propagandists on the labor side brand the Taft-Hartley Act as the "slave labor law" —thus returning the compliment.

Businessmen, trying to modify the laws against monopoly, plead for "fair trade" legislation, while automobile manufacturers over-sell their output by means of a "thrift plan." The American Medical Association torpedoed Mr. Truman's program for federal medical insurance by branding it "socialized medicine." "The displacement of the term 'insurance,' " said J. K. Galbraith, "by the term 'socialism' was a workmanlike achievement in the technique of argument."

Students of semantics call such terms *purr* words or *snarl* words. "Insurance" is of course a *purr* word, associated with home, mother, and security. "Socialism," at least in America, is a *snarl* word, associated with dividing up the wealth. Propagandists of all types, with advertisers in the lead, ransack

[7] Story from Schiller.

the dictionary for *purr* words to favor their product and *snarl* words to discomfit a competitor. The 1956 Mercury, we were assured on the radio, was the envied possessor of a "safety surge" engine. Boy! Surging power to pass anything on the road, yet perfectly safe!

SUGGESTIONS FOR A BULLETPROOF VEST

Some people seem to think that propaganda can do anything —including making water run uphill. If citizens are once exposed to a good dose of it, they are presumed to be done for. The first line of defense for citizens is the firm realization that this is not so. There are definite limits beyond which propaganda fizzles out. We will now briefly explore those limits, and offer some suggestions for personal protection. If words are bullets, every alert citizen should have handy a bulletproof vest.

WANTS AND NEEDS

Political propaganda has no power in itself; it is potent only when it connects with a deep human need shared by a great many people. When citizens feel insecure, confused, frightened, then political propaganda has a chance to bite. But if they feel prosperous, confident, and secure, all the wizards of the Kremlin cannot elicit much more than a yawn. The wizards on Madison Avenue can often persuade them to *buy* more stuff, however, by either rewards or threats.

Lenin had the overwhelming demand of the Russian people for peace to exploit. Hitler had the frustrations of the German people after World War I; McCarthy had the uncertainty of the American people in their country's new role as leader and banker for the world. The historian will record, however, that the frustrations of the American people, fully employed and prosperous in the 1950's, were shallow compared to those of the German people in the 1920's, or the Russian people in 1917.

PROMISES ARE NOT ENOUGH

Propaganda, even if addressed to mass wants, cannot continue to exert an effect by words alone. Sooner or later there must be *acts* to back up the words. Here is an example:

The Soviet delegate at a UN meeting on Indonesia once delivered the standard tirade against America. The delegate from India retorted: " The Soviet Union has done practically nothing to help this region, and has attributed malicious motives to other countries that have helped." While American counter-propaganda had been feeble compared to the blasts from Moscow, the tangible *acts* of America, expressed in foreign aid programs, had done more to hold friends than all the words in the dictionary. "In the final analysis," says Thomas Wilson, who covered the story for the *Reporter*, "the Communist system cannot deliver what it promises to deliver, and therein lies the fundamental weakness of the propaganda."[8]

Studies by Clyde Kluckhohn and his staff, at the Russian Research Center at Harvard, have suggested that Moscow's internal propaganda is losing some of its bite; the customers are getting bored with dialectial materialism. A serious limitation is that the lies and doubletalk are so farfetched that presently they are no longer believed by objective listeners, on the principle of "Wolf, Wolf!"

William Benton in the *Encyclopaedia Britannica* reports that today only about 10 percent of Moscow's internal publicity seeks to inculcate Communist doctrine. The other 90 percent aims to encourage technical proficiency, and especially to promote professional careers for bright youngsters. Already

[8] Russia, following the "new look," is stepping up her promises, and possibly her deliveries of tangible goods. The situation needs watching.

Russia is graduating more scientists and technicians than the U.S. Not more Marxism but more *managers* seems to be the present goal. Can the managers really compete with the West if they lack access to free inquiry and the scientific spirit? "In my judgment they are succeeding to an alarming degree," says Mr. Benton.

Political propaganda campaigns, no matter how expensive, eye-filling, and noisy, will not get far unless they (1) connect with a mass need, and (2) produce deeds to go with the words. They may also defeat their ends if they reach the height of total incredibility. The Russian educational drive for competent managers and technicians is something else again, and should bear the most careful examination. We would be very foolish to write it off as "mere propaganda."

SEMANTIC ARMOR

Bulletproof vests can be made from knowledge of how political propagandists operate, what techniques they use, the scapegoats they create, and the doubletalk they manufacture. This chapter has attempted to supply a little of this knowledge for the reader, and help to armor him for tomorrow's headlines.

An understanding of semantics also helps. Semantics, defined as "the systematic study of meaning," is useful, not only in analyzing the propagandists' talk, but in going behind the talk to the motives. It helps us to check abstract terms with concrete events, to dissolve word magic, to distinguish a fact from a value judgment. It exposes cases of guilt by verbal association, and enables one to trace the staircase of spurious identification. It locates black-or-white reasoning, and aids intelligent listening—the other half of talking. Semantics teaches us to watch our prejudices, and to take our exercise in other ways than jumping to conclusions. Semantics is the propagandist's worst friend.

22

The Life of Reason

ONE OF Kipling's characters says bitterly of another: "He thinks nobody thinks but himself." But isn't that true of most of us? We freely admit that some people have more expert knowledge of, say, the inside of the atom, or the inside of a motorcar. But when it comes to over-all judgment and plain common sense—what's the matter with everybody anyway?

Presumably we need this defense of the ego, lest we look into the abyss of all we do not know, and give up the struggle altogether. Presumably some readers of this book, however, take an interest in strengthening their reasoning apparatus— even though it is better than most people's! They see—as your author has seen in his own thinking—that there is room for improvement. Not much, perhaps, but a little.

REVIEW OF THE TOOL-MAKERS

In this brief account of everyday logic I have been chiefly concerned with certain common barriers to thinking. The pursuit of understanding, we have noted, is not a clear and open road. At least thirteen fallacies block the path. Some, like two-valued reasoning, are due in part to the structure of the language we use; in effect they have been built in. Others are due to local custom, such as the American awe of statistics, or to haste or laziness—for instance, substituting a "self-evident truth" for independent thought.

In the course of identifying the fallacies I have told many

stories, some of them perhaps amusing, but not intended merely to entertain. There are sharp tools here for tackling serious problems, both personal and social; tools to cut out the verbal underbrush, weapons to defend oneself against the special pleaders, who, with all the mass media at their command, keep us under continual attack . . . buy my soap, buy my candidate, buy my ideology!

The first tool-makers were the Greeks, and the master armorer was Aristotle. With the laws of thought and the syllogism, he made a magnificent beginning. His followers converted the knowledge into a "self-sealing" doctrine, and there substantially it stayed for two millennia. It took Galileo and Bacon, fortified with instruments and experiments, to break out of the logic of the classicists, and inaugurate the new logics and mental tools of modern science.

Only a superman can hope to master all the new tools. The wayfaring thinker can be aware, however, that they are on the bench, ready to hand. Some he can use without difficulty to deepen his understanding. He can apply semantics, developed principally by laymen for the layman, and not so hard to grasp as cybernetics, say, or the latest refinements in symbolic logic. No semanticist can ever be made the innocent victim of verbal brain washing. I will not go so far as to say that his brain is unwashable, only that its structure is tough.

PLAYING THE GAME

There is no reason why entertainment cannot be combined with understanding. The Liebers play a game they call "logical boners," in which they take samples from the news, the radio, the books they are reading, and analyze the errors. A fertile field for boners, as noted earlier, is the correspondence columns. Here citizens often work off their aggressive feelings about current events—"This is an outrage," they say, "*be-*

cause. . . ." In the analysis of that because, the student of logical fallacies can pursue his subject with both amusement and profit.

J. B. Priestley, after reading the papers in Texas, was somewhat more than amused when he said:[1]

Alongside these satirical columns in the Texas newspapers were letters from readers that were terrifying in their complacent ignorance. . . . Their writers argued as if they were living on the back of the moon. To them China was not a huge ruin of an Empire where armies had been wandering for years, but some little thing Alger Hiss or somebody had slipped to the Reds as a present. War was to be avoided by threatening with total destruction everybody who did not agree with the folks in Eagle Pass. . . .

REASON AND EMOTION

Let us go back to the question with which this book opened: Do we use our reason only to support our prejudices? After years of experience as an industrial psychologist, the late Dr. Stanley G. Law found himself in at least partial agreement with Bernard Shaw.[2] We are much more inclined to do what we feel like doing, he says, and then bring reason into play to justify the action. In the course of his duties as an industrial consultant, Dr. Law would interview an employee in this fashion:

"How did you feel about the foreman ordering you to shovel the two tons of sand?"

"I thought since he was boss I should do it," the man would reply.

"Yes, but how did you feel about it?"

"Well, I thought I ought to do it."

"That's what you thought, but how did you feel?"

[1] *Journey Down a Rainbow* (Harper, 1956).
[2] *Fundamentals of Industrial Behavior.* Paper presented before the Industrial Hygiene Foundation, November 16, 1955, by Dr. Christopher Leggo.

"I felt like ramming the shovel down his blankety blank throat!"

Dr. Law observed clinically that such an outburst "can have an excellent therapeutic effect." He went on to note that we accept an idea—when we do accept it—in one of two ways, intellectually or emotionally. If we are really to act on it, it must get into the nervous system, the emotions. Intellectual acceptance elicits a nod and the word "yes," but little compulsion to do anything about it. Intellectual assent can be immediate, while emotional acceptance usually requires time, and considerable repetition of the idea.

Anyone who undertakes to write about logic and reason needs to allow for this penetrating analysis. The hope of devoting ourselves to the unremitting life of reason is dim. But note the word "unremitting." The hope of sharpening the reasoning faculty, and even combining it with emotion from time to time, is somewhat brighter. One can become excited in tracking down an idea, as well as in tracking down one's next meal. For instance, I trust that I am exercising my mind in this study of logical fallacies, but I am also involved emotionally. Anybody who seriously writes a book becomes emotionally involved. Harsh and unjust words by a reviewer can be like the lash of whips.

Reason and emotion, as abstract terms, may seem separate and opposite, but in common experience they are closely related. A not unfair analogy might be the relation of the steering mechanism of a car to its engine. Without energy derived from feeling, the motor, we lack the power to solve problems—personal or general. Without the ability to think objectively and see clearly, the steering wheel, we are more likely to end in a ditch than to reach our destination. Freud and his successors showed plainly the source of mental energy in egotistical and inner drives, as well as the dangers of rationalizing our desires through wishful thinking.

Despite strong emotional drives, we remain the most logical of earth's creatures, and have survived more by our wits than our brawn. It is quite possible that the use of one's wits for survival can be extended. It would seem, indeed, that it must be extended, to cope with the thermonuclear problems which lie ahead.

Sir George Thomson, physicist and Nobel prize winner, is optimistic about this.[3] There are indications, he says, that we are very far from using our full mental potentialities. Consider infant prodigies and lightning calculators. "It is not obvious why everyone should not be able to do these things, and it looks as though there might be other similar faculties that could be made general if one knew how." Maybe only geniuses, he says, think freely and naturally. "The future will see . . . men's brains released from a tangle of hindrances that come from wrongly sorted impressions or barriers that have been set up."

Hindrances, wrong impressions, barriers—what better names could we find for fallacies in reasoning? The time may be nearer than we imagine when we shall break through the mental barriers, as a jet breaks through the barrier of sound.

[3] *The Foreseeable Future* (Cambridge University Press, 1955).

Appendix

Classification of Logical Fallacies

The classification follows the article on "Fallacies" in the *Encyclopaedia Britannica*, 14th Edition, Volume 9, page 55. This is the shortest and simplest list I have found. I have amplified the description of a fallacy now and then, and added occasional illustrations.

"An argument may be fallacious in *matter* (i.e., misstatement of facts), in *wording* (i.e., wrong use of words), or in *process of inference*." Fallacies are here classified accordingly as:

I. *Material*—having to do with facts.

II. *Verbal*—having to do with use of words.

III. *Logical* or *Formal*—having to do with drawing inferences.

These broad classes are then subdivided by the *Britannica* into:

I. Material Fallacies

1. *Fallacy of accident.* Confusing what is accidental with what is essential.

2. *Over-generalizing,* or *secundum quid.* Fallacy of arguing from special case to general rule with not enough cases to warrant a generalization. Or, *per contra,* arguing from general rule to special case, when the rule does not fit.

3. *Irrelevant conclusion,* or ignoring the issue *(ignoratio elenchi).* Instead of keeping to the issue, the arguer seeks to gain his point by diverting attention to irrelevant considerations. A long list is possible. The *Britannica* includes:

a. Argument *ad hominem*—attacking the character of the person defending the issue.

b. *Ad populum*—appeal to the sentiments of the crowd.

c. *Ad baculum*—appeal to fear.

d. *Ad verecundiam*—appeal to revered authority or "conventional propriety."

4. *Begging the question,* or *petitio principii.* This fallacy includes arguing in a circle *(circulus in probando),* whereby a conclusion is supposed to be demonstrated by inserting the conclusion into the premises. "Jeremy Bentham points out that this fallacy may lurk in a single word, e.g., if a measure were condemned simply on the ground that it is un-English"—or un-American.

5. *Fallacy of the consequent.* Assuming that if a man is a drunkard he becomes destitute, and then proceeding to argue that if a person is destitute he must be a drunkard.

6. *Fallacy of false cause,* or *non-sequitur.* Basing a conclusion on insufficient or incorrect reasons. (This applies, one would think, to *all* fallacies.)

7. *Post hoc ergo propter hoc: "After this, therefore because of this."* If event B comes after event A in time, then A is assumed to be the cause of B. If an eclipse of the sun is followed by the loss of a battle, the eclipse is assumed to be the cause of the defeat. *Per contra,* the cause of the victory for the other side.

8. *Fallacy of many questions,* or *plurium interrogationum.* Forcing two or more questions into one illegitimate question, e.g., "Have you stopped beating your wife? Answer yes or no."

II. Verbal Fallacies

1. *Equivocation.* Using one word in two or more senses, e.g.:

All fair things are honorable.
This woman is fair.
Therefore, she is honorable.

In America equivocation is usually called doubletalk.

2. *Amphiboly.* Fallacy due to use of inaccurate grammar, e.g., "They only voted last week" seems to mean they spent the entire week in a voting booth. (All they did last week was vote.)

3. *Composition.* A form of equivocation where terms are confused. What is true of a part is supposed to be true of the whole.

4. *Division.* The converse of *composition.* It concludes that what is true of a whole is also true of its parts, e.g.:

The U.S. believes that nations ought to disarm.
The U.S. is a nation.
Therefore, the U.S. should disarm—alone.

5. *Accent.* Fallacy due to emphasizing the wrong word in a sentence. This usually happens in speaking, not in writing, and accounts for much semantic confusion, intentional and otherwise.

6. *Figure of speech.* Misinterpretation of a form of expression, e.g., the phrase "bull in a china shop" has been known to insult Chinese delegates in the United Nations.

III. LOGICAL OR FORMAL FALLACIES

These are fallacies which violate the formal rules of the syllogism, and include:

1. *Fallacy of four terms, quaternio terminorum.* A formal syllogism can contain only three terms. Thus:

If A is taller than B
And B is taller than C
And C is taller than D
Then A is taller than D.

This syllogism is true, but it has four terms and is not allowed in the logic of the classicists.

2. *Fallacy of the undistributed middle term.* In a deductive syllogism, the middle term must be generalized or "distributed" at least once. It must also disappear in the conclusion. Usually it is generalized in the major premise, in order to include the middle term in the minor premise, e.g.:

Some carpenters are German.
Willy is a carpenter.
Therefore, Willy is German.

"All carpenters" would generalize the major term.

3. *Fallacy of illicit process of major or minor term.* The conclusion asserts more than the premises warrant.

All children are innocent.
No grownups are children.
Therefore, no grownups are innocent.

4. *Fallacy of negative premises.* Both premises cannot be negative, or you may reach an absurd conclusion, e.g.:

No snow is hot.
No rice is snow.
Hence, no rice is hot.

This completes the *Britannica's* list. It comprises three over-all classes, and twenty-one fallacies under them: eleven material, six verbal, and four formal. The last group is highly technical, applying primarily to the formal syllogism, and can be indefinitely extended. Frye and Levi in *Rational Belief,* for instance, list eighteen formal fallacies, including such collector's items as "Conversion of O proposition," and "Denying a disjunct." The journeyman thinker has little to gain by memorizing Section III.

It was from the *Britannica's* Sections I and II that I began the selection of the thirteen fallacies with which this book is mainly concerned. I then added certain others not catalogued by the classicists, but painfully evident to the layman, such as black-or-white reasoning and false analogies.

The *Britannica* list, condensed as it is, should give the reader a fair idea of the difficulties encountered in trying to identify and classify logical fallacies.

Suggested List for
Further Reading

Beardsley, Monroe C., *Thinking Straight* (Prentice-Hall, 1950).

Bridgman, Percy, *The Logic of Modern Physics* (Macmillan, 1932).

Chase, Stuart, *Power of Words* (Harcourt, Brace, 1954).

Cohen, Morris R. and Nagel, Ernest, *Logic and the Scientific Method* (Harcourt, Brace, 1934).

Doob, Leonard, *Public Opinion and Propaganda* (Holt, 1948).

Evans, Bergen, *The Natural History of Nonsense* (Knopf, 1946).

Frye, Albert Myrton and Levi, A. W., *Rational Belief* (Harcourt, Brace, 1941).

Hayakawa, S. I., *Language in Thought and Action* (Harcourt, Brace, 1949).

Howe, Quincy, *The News and How to Understand It* (Simon & Schuster, 1940).

Huff, Darrell, *How to Lie with Statistics* (Norton, 1954).

Lee, Alfred McClung, *How to Understand Propaganda* (Rinehart, 1952).

Lieber, Lillian and Hugh, *Mits, Wits and Logic* (2nd edition; New York: Galois Institute, Brooklyn, 1954).

Planck, Max, *The Philosophy of Physics* (Norton, 1936).

Robinson, James Harvey, *The Mind in the Making* (revised edition; Harper, 1950).

Ruby, Lionel, *The Art of Making Sense* (Lippincott, 1954).

Schiller, F. C. S., *Formal Logic* (London: Macmillan, 1931).

Young, J. Z., *Doubt and Certainty in Science* (Oxford, 1951).

Index

209

71 72 73 20 19 18 17 16 15 14 13